THE LEADERSHIP WOW FACTOR

3 Secrets to Elevate Your Impact,
Influence and Career

Tara Fennessy

10-10-10
Publishing

The Leadership 'WOW' Factor
www.leadershipwowfactor.com
Copyright © 2019 TARA FENNESSY

ISBN: 9781696538008

Publisher
10-10-10 Publishing
Markham, ON
Canada

Published in UK, USA & Canada

Table of Contents

I dedicate this book to my amazing children, Mikayla, Cameron and Charlie, without whom this would have been written and published much earlier!

To them, my awesome godchildren, my niece and nephew, whose energy, potential and life ahead excite me as future leaders.

To my parents, Sasha, Alison, Anne and Fiona for their never-ending support and belief in me.

With thanks to all my clients, as every conversation has mattered, raised my game and helped me to help them and others to be their best.

Grandad Pat, whose passing inspired me to get started and write this book.

Finally, in memory of my Uncle Brian, his wise advice of working hard, having common sense and a little bit of luck continues to guide my cousins and me.

About The Author

Awarded 'Best International Leadership Development Coach' by New York Times bestselling authors Jack Canfield and Raymond Aaron, Tara has been at the forefront of the leadership development sector for more than a decade. Currently, Tara is the managing director of Leadership Skills Training Limited, whose vision is "Best Bespoke Leadership Development Experience."

She is proud to have won Aquisition International's 2019 Leading Leadership Training and Coaching consultancy of the year, and Business Excellence 2018's Training Consultancy Firm of the Year.

The award-winning author and leadership master coach currently lives in the UK and travels regularly across the world, conducting masterclasses and coaching programmes to help global businesses develop their talent to achieve personal and business objectives.

Tara has worked across multiple industries and countries, helping emerging talent straddle the *ladder gap,* and supporting leaders at promotion and transition times.

She has loved working with her team at SMEs and Multinationals, and running their *Present with Impact* and *Lead with Impact* masterclasses.

Tara has also created the industry-leading Pulse Coaching Programme, and more recently, the blended and bespoke *WOW Your Presentations* and *WOW Your Leadership* digital experiences.

With this, her first book, Tara has shared her years of experience and in-depth insights that have helped many business leaders and their teams across the world accelerate their impact, influence, and careers.

When not pulling her hair out looking after two teenage boys and escaping to visit her daughter at university, Tara can often be found re-calibrating with a Malibu and diet coke planning her next holiday!

Foreword

Have you have ever felt slighted by your end results when you tried to assume a leadership role? Have you wanted to be a leader because you saw what needed to be done, but were unable to reach your leadership potential? If so, *The Leadership WOW Factor* is the book for you.

Numerous books have been written about leadership, with numerous theories and opinions. But ultimately it is up to you to choose how you want to lead, keeping in mind that if you are a good leader, you will always have the most profound impact, with the right message. You will know your audience, and will adapt your style to influence everyone around you, not only personally, but also professionally.

You may currently engage with leaders all the time. You may have been captivated by the vision of a leader and wished you could steal just one ounce of their passion and clarity. You may have wanted, and still want, to inspire your team, your boss or your clients, but you just can't figure out how to do it successfully.

That is why I am so excited to endorse this book. Over the last 25 years, author Tara Fennessy has trained, facilitated, coached, inspired, motivated, and transformed many aspiring business leaders and entrepreneurs to start functioning with the right skills and attitude, by showing them how to put the skills into effect rather than just consuming the knowledge and inching toward being a leader at a snail's pace!

Tara has found a way to make you want to learn more about your own inherent leadership skills and qualities. Her friendly and conversational tone will win you over, and her demonstrated acumen on the subject will excite you.

After reading this book, you will be empowered to begin your "treasure hunt" to find how these secrets will apply to your life and help achieve career defining success.

Raymond Aaron
New York Times Bestselling Author

Chapter 1

Introduction to WOW

"Leadership and learning are indispensable to each other."
– John F. Kennedy

For more than 20 years, I have been fascinated by the question: "How do people get promoted?"

More precisely, how do they get the top jobs and become leaders? Earlier on in their careers, most people get hired or promoted based on their CV and their performance in the job, but as they get nearer to the top, they find it increasingly difficult to climb that promotional ladder. It's what I call the *ladder gap*. The ladder gap is also common with people new to leadership positions: what got them there isn't often what makes them successful in their new role.

To be a successful business leader and straddle the ladder gap, companies expect you to be a brand ambassador, set the vision, deliver profitable growth through great teams, develop long-term and short-term relationships, seize opportunities and lead change, develop and coach the next generation, gain operational expertise in a number of disciplines, drive strategic initiatives, communicate in a clear and compelling way, own your career development, provide relevant insight and manage risk appropriately.

1

It's a lot to live up to, particularly when at the same time you're being challenged hard and are expected to be strong in standing up for what you believe is right—often without much support. My aim is for this book to help prepare you and support you through this journey.

It's like there's a missing rung in the career ladder, from junior leadership positions to senior leadership positions. Those willing to self-reflect, self-develop, get support and grow, successfully reach the top rung easier and quicker.

They learn to be their best, consistently, and adapt their style where necessary.

Over the years, I have been invited to join or consult on many promotional panel interviews, and have asked over 200 main board directors a critical question: "What most impresses you?" Or, significantly, "What least impresses you?"

None of their responses, surprisingly, relate specifically to getting the job done. Whilst there are obviously a range of answers, they do fall into three main themes:

Firstly, you need to be able to reinforce or *crystallise* the contribution you make in your role by communicating clearly and connecting with people, – from your boss to your peers and your stakeholders. Being able to simultaneously communicate clearly and connect to impress is the key to the power of what I call *connecticating*.

Most of my clients love this word, and they understand its meaning straight away, but some don't. I have challenged them to think of a better word, but I am still waiting!

(On a similar note, and of great importance, is another term, coined by Lord Bamford of the JCB dynasty, which is one of my favourite quotes: *"Don't complicate; simplicate."*)

Secondly, you need to set an inspiring vision and take people with you; you need to make your job look easy, not like hard work, and ideally cultivate a positive reputation so that people know about you before you enter the room.

Thirdly, being really good at your job gets you so far, but as you get closer to those senior management, director, or partner positions, you need to really stand out. In all organisations, but particularly large global corporates, most people unknowingly have adapted their style to fit in. This means that they don't stand out from the crowd or show leadership maturity or readiness.

My business, Leadership Skills Training, has a track record of helping over 5,000 people secure promotion, land their dream role and land with impact in a new leadership position. I have done this by helping them create the Leadership WOW Factor, the secrets of which I will share with you in this book.

Some people get leadership positions but fail to adapt and feel comfortable in their new role. They may fall short of the heightened expectations of the business—expectations that are so much higher in the senior positions.

One of the critical reasons why people do not progress is that they prioritise their *job*, not their career. They are so busy doing day-to-day tasks, or delivering deadlines, that they are then surprised, shocked, and sometimes devastated when they realise that not having devoted time to develop, reflect, and have conversations with stakeholders, has prevented them from climbing the next rung.

If this resonates with you, don't lose heart—you are the person who can get you there, by being the very best version of yourself. The following chapters provide the tips, tools, techniques, and advice to show you how.

If you are serious and committed to getting promoted, landing with impact in a new role, or getting your leadership mojo back—and are ready to put in the time and effort—the following three secrets can skyrocket you to where you want to be. They are summed up neatly, as *WOW*:

- **W**hat's your impact?
- **O**rbit effect
- **W**hat's most crucial?

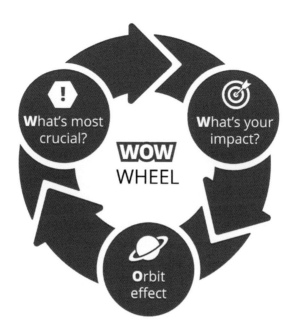

These three simple secrets—cornerstones, if you prefer—will elevate YOUR impact, influence, and career.

Throughout this book, I will expand on each of these three cornerstones, helping your leadership have the *WOW factor*.

So, what exactly do I mean by these three cornerstones of outstanding leadership? Outstanding leadership literally means: You stand out!

What's your impact? This is what it says on the tin. Not only do you need to crystallise your message and your vision, giving it clarity and punch so you can communicate and connect at the same time (the *connectication* I mentioned before), you also need to *be* your message. Live it and breathe it in everything you do and every conversation you have. That's how you take people with you and achieve results. To have great impact, you need to remember the ABC of leadership: Authenticity, Believability, and Credibility.

The *orbit effect* is about focusing your efforts on relationships with the people around you, and investing in them, from adapting your personal style so it resonates with their particular character traits, to expanding your network to engage with stakeholders outside of your daily routine.

What's most crucial? concentrates on how you can be your best, and the changes you can make in your life to ensure that you are always giving—and people are consistently seeing—the best you. It's also about nailing down your priorities, and reflecting on what is important to you, your achievements, and goals for the future. Equally, it recognises that you are not an island; the contribution of your team, and collaborating across the business, is crucial, and something you can influence with a little time and effort.

To master the cornerstones, you will need to find an approach that suits you. It may often push you out of your comfort zone. Don't panic; this is a good thing and will help your career. Each time you step outside your comfort zone, your new experiences mean your comfort zone expands and your resilience builds, so the next time you confront the same issue, it is now inside your comfort zone.

I believe in possibilities, joining your future dots, and accelerating your leadership growth journey—it's what my clients call *tough Tara love*. Outside your comfort zone is where you'll find *your* leadership WOW factor.

It's what gives you confidence and courage—two vitally important traits of a leader with the WOW factor.

My proven approach is founded on the principles of me being supportive but also challenging. Based on repeated feedback from my clients, I can tell you that no one will try harder than I do to help you look good and get promoted, to land your dream role, or elevate your impact and career prospects.

Remember, most people do not know these secrets (that's why they are secrets!), and not all of those who do will put them into practice.

So, if you are ready, read on, and you will discover the truths that every amazing leader already knows. Remember, they're based on tried and tested principles that really work. If you don't spend the time putting them into practice, you might find that one of the chapters in this book will haunt you if you fail to get promoted or advance in your career, and are told the reasons why.

I get my clients to make decisions and to take actions. You will need to do the same, which is why, at the end of each chapter, there are actions that you will need to take. I often raise my eyes upwards when I read this in other books, but there is scientific proof that writing something down really helps!

If you work through the actions in the next nine chapters, I promise that you will build all the skills to enable you to elevate your impact, influence, and career. It will also be a good thing to look back on and recognise the progress you will have made.

My gift to you is that you will be worth following. When you live the LEADERSHIP WOW FACTOR, people will want to be carried along on your journey. Using your learnings and next actions from this book, you will have the capability and knowledge to coach and develop your followers, sharing with them the secrets and power of WOW. Helping them will help you.

There is a reason why only 0.2 per cent of individuals reach the top echelons of business.

Are YOU ready to join them?

To start your journey, please start by taking some time to reflect and tick the boxes in the columns that are appropriate to you.

Wherever you are starting from, I can and will help you elevate your impact and influence in these areas, but **YOU** need to put in the time and effort—together, we can do this.

Three to six months is a realistic timeframe for there to be an authentic and noticeable difference in all these areas. My coaching programmes last six months, and my clients always have phenomenal results in accelerating their career and impact.

If you would like to join our online coaching programme for additional support to keep you accountable, spur you on, and give you bespoke guidance, check out www.leadershipwowfactor.com.

YOUR NEXT ACTIONS

	Nothing in last 12 months.	Once in last 12 months.	Twice in last 12 months.	Three times or more in last 12 months.
How often do you think about your career development?				
How often have you prioritised your career development?				
How many career development conversations have you had?				
How much positive feedback have you had on clarity of your communication in emails, conversations, presentations, updates?				
How many times have you consciously attempted to articulate your purpose, vision, strategy and legacy as best you can?				
How often have you received feedback on your personal impact?				
How often have you asked for feedback on your personal impact?				
How often have you consciously adapted your style to get the best out of someone?				
How often have you reached out to someone outside your business area and tried to influence them?				
How often have you initiated a conversation about one of your business leader's priorities/ challenges?				
How often have you contributed to something outside of your area for the broader business benefit?				
How many team building activities/meetings/ away days have you had?				
How many times have you asked your team – what do you need from me?				
How many times have you asked for or received feedback on your leadership style?				
Have you spent time working on any of your development areas?				
How many networking events have you attended?				
How many times have you been asked to speak internally or externally?				
How many times have you spoken externally?				
How many times have you posted on social media in a professional context?				
How many times have you reached out to connect on LinkedIn or updated your profile?				
How many times have you looked at your calendar and asked yourself - am I correctly balancing my time?				
How often have you paused and reflected on your priorities?				
Totals	Score zero for each tick.	Score one for each tick.	Score two for each tick.	Score three for each tick.

Less than 35: You need this book! There is a whole range of opportunities you're currently missing out on! This book will elevate your career.

35-50: You're on the way! This book will accelerate your impact, influence and career.

Over 50: You're doing well. Time to be your best and reach the top of the ladder.

Secret 1 - the first W in **W**OW

What's your Impact?

Chapter 2

Know Your Message

"Great leaders are almost always great simplifiers,
who can cut through argument, debate and doubt to offer
a solution everybody can understand."
— General Colin Powell

In my many interviews with leaders, the most consistent reasons they give for people not being promoted is lack of personal impact, not being able to get to the point or land their message, or articulate their contribution.

The real job of a leader is to inspire people to create a better future. Effective communication is a leader's most critical skill to influence others to do this. That's why the first secret—the first **W** in WOW— is **W**hat's your impact?

Great leaders communicate memorable messages.

To elevate your impact, you must know your message.

Having crystal clear leadership messages really elevates your impact. It is essential you know your messages. One dictionary definition of message is *"a communication from a prophet or preacher, believed to be inspired by God."* Remember: It is your job to inspire people with your purpose, vision, strategy, and legacy. Now, more than ever, people want to work for someone they admire and who is trying to create a better future, and that together your legacy is something that makes a difference that we can all be proud of.

You must be able to crystallise and articulate your personal contribution, your previous achievements, your priorities and challenges in the role, and why YOU are uniquely placed to solve and handle them.

In preparation for an interview or promotion, think of yourself as a vehicle that can help get the business to their desired destination, whether it be gaining a bigger market share, increasing sales, developing innovative products, beating the competition, or breaking into new markets.

In any of these scenarios, having and displaying confidence are key, and presenting yourself is your most visible skill. People put a question mark over your ability to do a job well if you cannot present well, but the opposite works too: If you have a clear message and can present it confidently and clearly, people will assume you are good at doing your job. Not very fair, I know, but definitely true. I will teach you to elevate your impact and give you the ability to be in the top five per cent of presenters, saving you time preparing, and in turn, making you feel a lot more confident.

The first thing you need to consider, when you are presenting, is whom you are presenting to.

WHO IS YOUR AUDIENCE?

This sounds obvious, but it is rarely done well. The first thing you need to do is focus on your audience or interviewer, and ask yourself, "What do they want to hear?" NOT, "What do I want to say?"

Read that last sentence again. There is a vast difference, and it's the most critical thing people consistently let themselves down on, not just at interview time but whenever they are presenting, whether to the board, in a town hall, or at a social event, and equally whether they are presenting ideas, updates, or pitching for work. There is a natural desire to make ourselves feel valuable by telling our audience everything we know about the subject; it justifies our presence, and makes us feel knowledgeable and good. However, what we need to do is help our audience with what they need to know and what they may need to do. Most people do not do this well. We also need to be aware of how they might be feeling so that we can take them with us and keep them listening.

Think about the following:

- Who will be there?
- How much do they know about my subject area?
- What is their attitude to me presenting, and do they have any preconceived ideas?

If your audience are all experts, then you will be okay keeping it technical. If there is a mixed level of knowledge in the room, which is quite likely the more senior you are, then you will not be okay keeping it all technical. Let me give you an example...

I recently worked with a doctor who was speaking at St Bartholomew's Hospital in London, and his subject was narcolepsy (a condition characterised by frequent and uncontrollable periods of deep sleep).

He said: "I have 90 doctors coming to see me. Six of them are leading experts on the subject and, by definition, know a lot about it, and I would quite like to impress them. The remainder are GPs (general practitioners) who know about as much as you do. My problem is that if I pitch it at a fairly high level, some people are going to get bored and end up looking out of the window, which will put me off. If I pitch it at a more basic level, the experts are going to be thinking: 'Who does he think he's talking to?' Either way, I'm stymied."

I explained that the best tip is to let your audience know that there is a mixed level of knowledge in the room. So, this is how he started: "Good morning, ladies and gentlemen. As you know, my subject today is narcolepsy, and I am delighted to have six leading experts with us today, and if they could just bear with me for a few moments, I will bring the rest of us up to speed on the basics of narcolepsy, and just how far we have got."

People in the audience typically don't take account of who is sitting next to them. This tip helps you to have impact in your very first sentence.

You also need to pay close attention to what the audience wants to hear from you.

If you can start by understanding where your audience's heads are at first, it is a lot easier to take them along with you later in the presentation. People decide in the first few sentences whether they are going to listen to you.

I worked with one of the directors from Unilever who was going up to Sunderland to speak to the workforce. He said he was going to talk about the big picture, where they were going, and "all that good stuff."

I suggested, that before he went, that he ring up a few of them (yes, ringing and speaking—not emailing—is often a better way to *connecticate*), and ask them what they might like to hear from him.

He came back to me the next day and was absolutely astounded by the responses he had got.

"They want to know when the pot holes in the road are going to be cleared up."

I asked him why.

"Because the pot holes in the road are causing the loaders to dip down, and the barrels are spilling off. They are also really concerned about when their new overalls are being delivered, and they have heard rumours that we are laying people off. We are not laying people off; we are recruiting at the moment. Tara, are you saying that I should not talk about the big picture, where we are going, and all that good stuff?"

My reply was clear: "No, by all means, but start from where their heads are at first."

Great leaders find out before a team meeting what the team would really like to hear. If you are presenting to a board of directors, you could contact them first, ideally speaking to them, or send a very brief email, simply headed, *Your Expectations*.

You could perhaps then write something along these lines: "I am presenting to the board next week on (your topic). Is there anything you are particularly concerned about or would like me to cover?"

Remember, most people don't make contact like this. How would you feel if someone asked you? Be brave – remember stretch yourself out of your comfort zone. Most people are impressed if they are asked for their thoughts or views, and actually look forward to the presentation more, as they know it's likely to be more relevant to them.

If you employ this technique, you'll already have impact before you walk in the room to start the presentation. The added benefit for you is that it can also calm your nerves and make you feel a lot more confident about what questions you may be asked.

How many people have you heard present in the last 12 months that have impressed you—really impressed you? Think about it...how many? Out of how many presentations in total? Probably at least a couple of dozen. Maybe if they had employed some of these simple, easy to achieve techniques, they would have impressed you more. The good news is—and this is really good news for you—it's not difficult to look good and really elevate your impact in this way.

So, for your audience, make sure you cover WIIFT: What's in it for them?

Walk a few miles in their shoes before you even start to think about what you will say. Find out some basic information that will help you consider their perspective:

- Who is your audience—their levels, knowledge, and experience?
- What time are you presenting? Are they giving up a break; is it close to lunch or home time?
- What is your audience doing or hearing before you present to them? It can have an impact.
- Who is presenting before you?

Pay particular attention to finding out who else is presenting if there is more than just you, especially if they are just before you. Contact that person and let them know that you're both presenting (when and where), and ask them what their message is and what they will be covering. There is nothing worse than waiting your turn and hearing someone else steal your thunder, or not hearing it, and presenting anyway, only to then unknowingly bore your audience with repetition.

So, you've thought about your audience; you are now ready for the next part of your presentation preparation.

HAVE A CLEAR MESSAGE

What is the one thing you want your audience to remember?

Picture someone who's been in your audience, meeting someone else and being asked how your presentation went. "Great," they tell them. "What was said?" they are asked. Your audience member replies, "Well, they said...." The next words that come out of their mouth are a measure of how well you have delivered your message, and how much impact it had. You can decide what impact is created by shaping these words. You do this by having a clear, concise message that everyone understands and remembers.

Decide to be clear: What is your message?

How do you do that? Here's the secret: It must be eight words or fewer—tough Tara love, indeed!

Not nine words, or ten, but eight. Think of any clear, concise message from any great speech or presentation:

- *"I have a dream."* – Martin Luther King
- *"This lady's not for turning."* – Margaret Thatcher
- *"We will fight them on the beaches."* – Winston Churchill

"I did not have sexual relations with that woman." – Bill Clinton (Notice, 9 words—not as impactful or believable!!)

Advertisement slogans work well with the rule too:

- "I'm lovin' it." (McDonald's)
- "Just do it." (Nike)

In fact, the holy grail of advertising slogans is 3 words.

It takes a lot of effort to get this right. Most people say, "I just want them to remember me," or, "I want them to feel that I can do the job," but these things are your purpose, not your message.

It is, of course, important to decide your purpose—are you presenting or communicating? Do you want to persuade them, motivate them, inspire them, or inform them? Do you need them to approve something or sign something off? Do you want to plant seeds for an upcoming opportunity?

BUT—*what is your message?*

I go back again to the critical question: What's the one thing you want them to remember?

If you can get the answer to that, in eight words or fewer, then you have done much better than most. This aim of eight words or fewer will become the focus of your presentation.

DO NOT START WORKING ON YOUR PRESENTATION UNTIL YOU HAVE DONE THIS.

A great way to work on the message for your presentation is again to think of two people discussing your delivery afterwards. If it's really good, then every person in the audience, when asked what message they got from it, would say the same eight words or fewer that you have just decided upon.

Ask yourself: Would you be happy to hear what they said your message was? Was it an accurate reflection of what you're trying to convey? Did it have impact? Did it have a WIIFT focus?

If you're not happy with what you think these answers would be, then you need to rethink your message.

Once you are clear on who your message is aimed at, and what your message is, you then need to start thinking about how you are going to organise your information and presentation, so that it is clear and holds people's attention.

HAVE A CLEAR STRUCTURE

Let's take an example. Let's say that you have decided your message is *Structuring for Success*.

Once you've decided on your message, it would be very easy to just randomly brain dump your thoughts, but the most efficient and effective way to think about your content is to decide on your structure.

The rule for doing this is to elevate your impact by having no more than three key areas, each of which reinforces your message.

Example:
MESSAGE: Structuring for Success
KEY AREAS: ONE GOAL   ONE PLAN   ONE TEAM

Can you see how this already has more impact than most presentations? Even two key areas can work. For example, you could use:

HOW TO GET YOUR CUSTOMERS
HOW TO KEEP THEM

HOW TO MAXIMISE MONEY COMING IN
MINIMISE THE MONEY GOING OUT

Other structures you might find useful

WHY	HOW	WHEN
PAST	PRESENT	FUTURE
PEOPLE	PRODUCT	PROFIT
PROBLEM	POSSIBILITIES	PROPOSAL

It doesn't have to be these; it can be any you choose but never more than three.

So, you have thought about your audience, you have your message/focus for your presentation, and you also have the structure.

Next, a really useful tip to help balance your presentation, in terms of content, is to have more impact with your audience.

YOUR TIMING

If your presentation is 20 minutes long, then you might decide that each of your three key areas are equally important, so perhaps you would spend six minutes on each of the key areas. That's 18 minutes in total, plus two minutes for your opening and conclusion, which we will cover later.

Many presenters don't get this balance right, or if they have planned it, they don't always stick to it. Often, they spend too much time on the area they know most about, and bore their audience to tears, and end up with them getting distracted and checking their phones. Remember to ask yourself, "Who is my audience?" What you say, and how much time you spend on each area, is driven by their needs.

In the example presentation, Structuring for Success, I had a forty-five minute slot. I spent ten minutes on ONE GOAL, twenty minutes on ONE PLAN (the most important bit for my audience), and ten minutes on ONE TEAM. That way, the key areas were balanced well for my audience, and I felt confident about this before I started preparing each section.

RECAP

Remember: To elevate your impact, you must know your message.
Know your audience.
Know your message.
Know your structure.
Know your timings.

Additional Resources:
www.leadershipWOWfactor.com/WOWyourPresentations

YOUR NEXT ACTIONS
Start preparing for an upcoming presentation using this template.

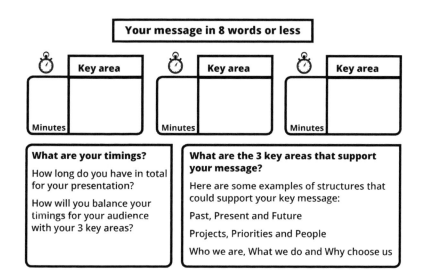

Chapter 3

Be Your Message

Leadership is a potent combination of strategy and character.
But if you must be without one, be without the strategy.
– Norman Schwarzkopf

Leaders' *Pulse* Rate

For the past 20 years, I have been pushing people hard to come up with not just what they think their message is, but also to combine it with what they know and feel, so that it becomes believable and powerful, not just for them but also for their audience.

Leaders must manage their messages. Organisations can sink into chaos when leaders do not manage what comes out of their mouths.

Leadership isn't easy, but vague, clichéd, and unclear messages make many leaders' jobs infinitely more difficult than they need to be.

Statements, like "Customers come first," and "Let's focus on the key priorities this quarter," are foggy, and they can mean different things to different people.

I also hear many leaders talk about vision, trust, loyalty, teamwork, focus, priorities, etc., without saying what they mean. We often ask the 12 attendees on our Lead with Impact workshop to describe what these words mean, and almost certainly, we get 12 different definitions.

If leaders themselves don't understand what these terms mean, and they also don't, or can't, explain them to their teams, it causes great confusion.

People tend not to ask leaders for clarification, for fear of looking stupid. They nod politely and assume everyone else understands what is meant, and fearing it's just them that are missing something. This results in inactivity, confusion, and/or mistakes.

I became more fascinated with this when I began to understand how the brain works.

I believe, to be at our best and to have the WOW factor, it helps to understand how the brain works, as this impacts all we come into contact with at home and at work.

Often, what comes out of leaders' mouths is what they are **thinking,** which comes from one part of the brain: the human or neomammalian part. It controls language, ideas, concepts, and artistic visions.

There are two other parts of our brains that leaders also activate.

The reptilian part gives us our instinct, dominance, and survival actions, without us having to think about it. It is what I call, **what they know.**

The mammalian part gives us our feelings and emotions. It records memories of behaviours that produced agreeable and disagreeable experiences, and is responsible for most of our emotions. It is also responsible for our compare and contrast mechanisms, which lead to value judgements. It controls a lot of our behaviour, if still somewhat unconsciously. It is what I call, **what we feel.**

My coachees learn to self-adjust their brain dial regularly, and that generally their WOW factor is 20% what they think, 40% what they feel, and 40% what they know more of this in Chapter 9, Know your Best).

People want to know what their leaders are really thinking and feeling, and why. When they get this and connect with it, they'll bend over backwards to help. In the absence of this connection, projects fail, time is wasted, and targets are not met. Individuals and teams are not aligned, politics and rumours abound, and talented people lose focus.

Imagine military leaders not communicating clearly! People will die if communication is not accurate and precise. Doctors, nurses, and surgeons use the same language so that everyone is clear in an emergency room. What comes out of their mouths is what they think, feel, and know. Everyone has a precise understanding of what they need to do, and are inspired to take the appropriate action.

Remember, the true purpose of leadership is to inspire people to create a better future. Leaders influence others by employing their most effective, visible, and critical skill: communication of their messages.

Messages can wield extraordinary influence. Great leaders communicate memorable messages.

Notice that Martin Luther King had a dream—not a plan or strategy. The words need to mean something to people. They need to be memorable. People need to believe in them.

I have seen companies, cultures, and people thrive when inspired by clear and defined communication. By contrast, when they lack this definition and communication, they flounder—basically because it is what a leader is thinking at a given time.

When leaders take time to explain what they mean explicitly (know their message), and implicitly (be their message through their behaviours), they can wield extraordinary influence. Improved performance and efficiency, better relationships, and clear feedback follow. As a rough guide, knowing your message and being your message is roughly 20% what you think, 40% what you feel, and 40% what you know.

I want people to know what you mean, what you think, and how you feel, so that they work with you to achieve your goals, and they do everything they can to make you all succeed as a team. You'll remember, from Chapter 2, about the importance of your message being memorable in 8 words or less. You want to influence what people say about you and what your message is. You can achieve this by knowing your message and being your message. This impact cascades if others understand - and repeat - your words.

Time for tough Tara love. It requires patience and effort.

I believe there are 5 critical steps leaders need to work through in order to make their messages have the WOW factor. These steps are the basis for most conversations, meetings, sales, objective settings, and even emails.

It's what I call your leader's PULSE rate.

P = Purpose – What is it that you REALLY do?
U = Uniqueness – How are you uniquely placed to deliver that?
L = Leadership vision – What is your leadership vision?
S = Solution – What is your strategy to deliver your vision?
E = Excellence – What are you putting into best practice that will become common practice?

Your PULSE helps you connect and communicate— – *connecticate* with clarity, confidence, and courage. It's how you show up.

When the answers to the questions come from what you think, feel, and know, it's strong, repeatable, and rhythmical. If it's a healthy rhythm, and you really do know your message, and you are your message, the elusive leadership WOW factor is in your reach.

Purpose

You often hear people talk about their purpose, including motivational speaker, Simon Sinek, who stresses the need to "know your why." He believes that in addition to knowing how important the "how" and "what" are, it is truly the "why" that sets the passionate leaders and change agents apart.

Purpose is essential, and I think, combined with all the steps I am going to take you through, it will increase your impact, influence, and credibility.

So, if I am at a networking event, and someone asks me what it is that I do, I could respond by saying: "I am a Director/a trainer/a consultant/a coach."

Unenthralled by my job title talk, people may continue to chat to me for a few minutes, but will then politely excuse themselves.

You may have had situations where corporate "blah blah blah" has come out of your mouth when you are describing what you do.

Know your audience: What you're saying needs to impress them. What is the difference you make? What is it you really do? How can it relate to them?

Before I realised the impact of this, I used to say that I am a leadership coach.

Now when someone asks me what I do, I reply: "I help leaders have the WOW factor."

Guess which reply peaks their interest.

Also, I never start a sales conversation about my business. Invariably, people start a conversation with me instead. For example, in conversation, they will often describe a challenge where they are not having enough impact or influence. I offer them some on-the-spot advice, and then they ask me to come in and chat to them more.

People don't care if you are an expert marketeer, or if you are a transformation guru. They care about your outcomes and what's in it for them!

Your purpose does not just apply to how you introduce yourself at networking events, but how you position yourself internally and externally, online and offline!

What is your purpose?

I can help you with this now, but I would suggest that you stop reading for 5 minutes, go and get yourself a drink—water, tea, coffee, or even a glass of wine or a beer—go somewhere relaxing, get comfortable, empty your head for a minute, and take a few breaths. In my experience, we can quickly get past the corporate "blah blah blah" if you do this. Don't just think the answer; we need to bridge what your head, heart, and gut say—what you think, know, and feel it is that you REALLY do.

Connecting to your core purpose is extremely powerful. You should be coming up with something no one has said before.

Again, remember—as ALWAYS—eight words or less make it very powerful.

Let's ask some questions:

1. What are the outcomes of what you do?

It may help to break it down by asking yourself the following:

What verb really gets the essence of describing what you do for someone?

Do you create, transform, inspire, design, or pioneer? Don't just think it—say it out loud.

This may take you a few attempts. When you get the right word, you'll feel it, and you'll know this is what you really do. In fact, you love doing it. I know that I really help. I love helping people.

Clients, family, and friends always say, "Tara really helped me."

Remember that when you get these critical messages right, they become what other people say about you too.

2. What do you do?

I help people understand the power of their messages, and increase their personal impact.

3. Whom do you do it for?

Leaders

4. What's the result in terms of change or transformation?

The WOW factor

Do you see now how I got "I help leaders have the WOW factor?"

Here are some examples of companies' purposes that sum up perfectly what they do, who for, and the end result:

EY: Building a better working world
Tesco: Helping shoppers a little better every day
Tesla: Accelerate the world's transition to sustainable energy
TED: Ideas worth sharing

Uniqueness

There may be many people in your organisation or industry who do exactly the same as you. Faced with competition all around, it's crucial to identify what sets you apart, which is where uniqueness comes in.

The one big question here is:

How are you uniquely placed to [insert your purpose here]?

So how am I uniquely placed to help leaders have the WOW factor?

I help them to know their message and be their message. No one else has said that or does that.

What's the one thing you are supremely qualified to do? What do others say about what you do?

Again, your answer should be unique—no one else will have said this combination of purpose and uniqueness. Maybe you have specific technical/industry experience, or a skill that makes you the industry expert, the go-to person, and the subject specialist.

Often, people do not know what makes them unique, as their uniqueness is what comes naturally to them.

Perhaps ask someone (ideally a trusted client or maybe a colleague): "What's unique about me?"

Better still, ask them how you are uniquely placed to (say your PURPOSE)!

Really try and reflect, and ask people who will help you identify your purpose.

It can lead to an important recalibration to helping you be your best, and have the leadership WOW factor.

One of my clients, Patrick, identified his purpose as "to guide our company to excite our customers."

He'd recently been promoted to commercial director in Prague, the first local director of a UK owned retailer.

His uniqueness was being born there, living there, and being the most senior local person. He understood their customers' habits, whilst simultaneously understanding which direction the business wanted to move toward.

To answer the question, "How am I uniquely placed to (purpose) 'guide our company to excite our customers,'" his answer (uniqueness) was: "Knowing the habits and history to drive evolvement."

The above demonstrates how Patrick was able to pinpoint, very succinctly, exactly what differentiates him from the pack (of UK leaders). He became their first local leader.

Leadership Vision

This is possibly the most important component of your PULSE.

When people are aligned to a vision, the possibilities are incredible. A great vision will guide and motivate people to grow and improve. It should provide hope in tough times, particularly when it is the result of living a company's purpose. A purpose is what you do every day. Your vision is where that will get you, and is, by nature, more futuristic.

Many company visions include numbers for example, i.e. £2bn in two years.

I think there needs to be a bit more feeling in a great vision so you can take people with you.

Mine is: the best bespoke leadership development experience.

A true vision provides focus for everyone.

You may know the story of President John F. Kennedy visiting **NASA** headquarters for the first time, in 1961, and asking the janitor/caretaker, "What do you do?"

"I am helping put a man on the moon," was the reply.

If something gets you closer to your vision, you do it; if it doesn't, you don't.

Is this helping put a man on the moon?

Yes, it is. Do it!

No, it doesn't. Don't!

A true vision also helps answer every question that might come up.

So, when my team and I were deciding on whether to offer an online version of our Present with Impact Masterclass, a two-day event we run for leaders, I asked, "Will it be the best bespoke online leadership development experience?"

We knew our clients wanted us to have more impact and more reach, as it becomes increasingly difficult to take multiple executives out of the office for two days.

So, we decided we would break the training down into five simple, five-minute lessons that would help you design, develop, and deliver a WOW presentation.

You would submit each step for personal review, feedback, and coaching.

You could also optionally (depending on your learning style) watch the lesson being taught to a live group.

We had the answer to my question: Yes, it would; no one else is doing that.

We won Business Excellence 2018's award for Training Consultancy Firm of the Year.

"When there is no vision, the people perish." – Proverbs 29.18

A great vision provides clarity, confidence, and courage for a leader, even during challenging times.

When a leader has this, the people and company do too!

If you can't see yourself winning that award, taking number one position in the market, getting your dream job, and feeling the pride and tears of triumph, it's unlikely you'll be able to lead yourself and others into victory. You must see it, smell it, taste it, hear it, and feel it in your gut.

Napoleon Bonaparte said: *"A leader is a dealer in hope."*

The skill to translate hope into a vision that becomes a reality is something you must develop.

I know it takes time to clarify your vision, but remember, it takes the same amount of time to dream big as it does to dream small! So, be big, be bold, and go for gold, the highest level you can achieve in your chosen field. Do you want to be the biggest, world class, award winning, #1 in UK, Europe, EMEA, or globally?

Solution

Once you have your vision, decide how you are going to get there. In other words, what is your strategy to deliver this vision?

So, for our WOW Your Presentations online course, our vision is to get you into the top five per cent of presenters. How are we going to achieve this?

Our solution/strategy for our online course, to deliver the best bespoke online leadership development experience, is: Learn it, See it, Do it.

Learn it – There are five modules, with a five-minute recording of each, where you learn how to wow your presentations.

See it – You can see each of the five modules being taught in our live masterclass.

Do it – For each module, you submit homework, which you will receive feedback on from your personal coach.

The above neatly clarifies our solution to making you a master of presenting. Think about your solution to getting where you want to be—can you describe it in three simple steps?

Excellence

What are you putting in as best (excellent!) practice that will become common practice? What will be there after you have gone? I remember one of my clients at JCB was for there to be a JCB machine on every building site in the world!

So, the Pulse for our online course is:

P: WOW your presentations in 30 minutes
U: Bespoke, facilitated and flexible experience
L: Get into the top five per cent of presenters
S: Learn it, See it, Do it
E: The first secret to elevate your impact, influence, and career

Let me share with you some of my clients PULSEs:

Rachel is a retail director for a home improvements UK chain, and her PULSE in that role is:

Purpose: To help shape the retail plan

Uniqueness: Able to influence the plan from every angle

Leadership Vision: Add brilliant value to the business

Strategy: Be highly collaborative, land right first time, simplicity in everything we do

Excellence (Legacy): High performing teams delivering brilliant work

She also has a PULSE for her role as a leader in the business:

Purpose: Create a buzz and belief to be brilliant
Uniqueness: Challenging and lifting others as I climb
Leadership Vision: Surrounded by brilliant people doing brilliant things
Strategy: Simplicity in all that we do, by setting tone & pace, and being decisive
Excellence: Inspiring others to be their best

My client, Patrick, who I mentioned earlier, had lost his mojo and was wondering if he was good enough or should leave. Defining the following PULSE allowed him to get back his energy and, within a year, he went on to become MD in one of his organisation's European countries:

P – Guiding our business to excite our customers
U – I know the habits and history to drive our evolvement
L – Central Europe's most trusted and innovative fresh food retailer
S – Optimise the range, Develop iconic products, Be decisively stable
E – Happy customers shopping more frequently

As these examples demonstrate, not only can you PULSE the specifics of your job, you can also PULSE your wider role as a leader in your business.

In fact, there are quite a few things you can PULSE; for instance, a project you are working on.

You can PULSE your achievements, which is great for your CV and interview preparation.

I did the latter with a client who was preparing for a big job interview at Amazon; we PULSE'd all his career achievements by answering the same pulse questions, and soon came up with a set of WOW answers that dazzled his interviewers who said it was best interview they'd ever had.

Next actions

PULSE your current role, your role as a leader in your business, a project you are working on, or one of your achievements.

Extra resources are available for free, at leadershipwowfactor.com/ wowyourbraindial, and leadershipwowfactor.com/wowyourpulse.

Purpose - What is it you really do?

_____
_____

Uniqueness - Why are you uniquely placed to do it?

_____
_____

Leadership - What is the vision?

_____
_____

Solution - What is your strategy?

_____
_____

Excellence - What will the legacy be?

_____
_____

Chapter 4

Know Your Impact

"Ninety percent of leadership is the ability to communicate something people want."
– Dianne Feinstein

By now, I hope you can see and understand the impact of crystallising your contribution, and structuring your critical leadership messages.

This will help provide the base and context for your presentations, conversations, proposals, and emails. Now you need to think about the impact of what comes after your message and structure—your content. Content isn't just about what you say but how you say it too—it's the cake with the icing, cherry, and sprinkles on top.

Frequently leaders talk theoretically, using jargon (what I call blah, blah, blah), and people listening switch off or are easily distracted— hardly conducive to help elevate your personal impact. Instead, they need to bring things to life, and win the hearts and minds of their team, peers, and internal and external stakeholders.

The Rule in Presenting

There's a rule in presenting that not only makes you more interesting and memorable; it also helps you demonstrate clarity and credibility.

Everything that you say and do in your presentation must reinforce your message and bring it to life. It's great you have your message now (eight words or less), but everything else must support it. When I hear most presentations, or someone explaining why they are best placed for a role, this does not happen—most people babble on.

There is one rule in presenting, which most people don't even know.

The rule is: **"Make a succinct point and then illustrate it."**

Keep your points succinct.

Your points reinforce your structure and should be mentioned solely for this purpose, and be appropriate for your particular audience.

Power point is often relied on heavily and is used in presentations in order for people to explain their points. Perhaps when there is a lot of technical or complicated data, it may play a role, but it should not be used as standard in most presentations.

You need to remember that you are presenting and not reading from a textbook. In fact, your audience can read slides for themselves, so you doing this is not adding value. Consider also that the more senior you are, the less you should rely on power point, as they have come to see and hear you present. Remember, visual aids should visually aid the audience and **not** the presenter!

It is much better to say to yourself, "What is my point?" and answer it in a succinct and simple way.

James, a client of mine, needed to speak to his board on digitalisation. He said to me: "Digitalisation is something important that some of our competitors are prioritising.

The processes, platforms, and cost means that it is a timely and expensive task, but one we should be considering if we want to be taken seriously in our market."

I asked him: "James, what's your point; what are you really trying to say?"

He said, "We need to digitalise or die." Much punchier!

In our Present with Impact master class, we explore this rule. We go around the room and get people to give it a go. If they don't think about what they really want to say, they tend to babble on. If they stop, think, and just reflect for a moment, and are guided, if necessary, with "What's your point?" then the next thing that comes out of their mouth is much more WOW.

You look much better at your job when you keep it simple, which is perfectly summed up by the acronym K.I.S.S.: Keep it simple speaker.

Unfortunately, most people lose impact by telling you too much; they think it impresses, but the opposite is true.

What about the second half of the rule?

Illustrate it.

This is essential. Using examples avoids ambiguity, and it holds people's attention.

People really relate to examples and evidence, which links them back to the point you want them to remember.

In James' example, his point was "digitalise or die." The example he used was: "Creating an app will grow market share by 15 per cent."

Can you see the difference there would be in his impact?

We will explore the skills for illustration next. So, how can you go about improving the way you illustrate your points? There are certain skills and techniques that everyone can adopt that will make your illustrations much more memorable.

You may recall that I mentioned the ability to *connecticate,* which is an important element of the leadership WOW factor. A great tip for connecticating and holding people's attention is to use proper nouns. Proper nouns are the names of persons, places, organisations, or product names, spelled with a capital letter. Proper nouns paint pictures in people's minds, which is vital given our brains are hardwired to remember pictures rather than words.

Think of someone you know who is good at telling stories. I bet they are good at describing where they are and whom they are with. Most people (particularly British) abstain from using names, as they think, if you do not know or will never meet someone, what's the point of using their name?

You'll notice now the proper nouns I use, and perhaps recall me mentioning Lord Bamford or JCB, Tesco, Unilever, and EY.

Rather than saying *in six months' time*, it is better to say May 2020.

I do appreciate that you may have client confidentiality, but where it is internal, in the public domain, or you can get permission, please use proper nouns; it makes a huge difference to holding people's attention. Beneficial for your confidence and your impact, using proper nouns is often when people who are listening to you will smile or nod. Let me be clear; I do not mean name-dropping for name-dropping's sake. Simply use them in the examples that illustrate your points.

Using proper nouns definitely adds to your impact, and can enhance your credibility.

Numbers, or data, in examples, also work well for holding audience's attention.

The Key for Persuasion

I previously asked the question, when talking about your purpose: Are you presenting or communicating? If you are trying to persuade people, remember this: Parallels persuade. Generally, people fear change; it's a natural and understandable response. If you can show where something has already been successful, they are then far more likely to go for it.

James' digitalisation point is a good example of using a parallel. He mentioned that one of their competitors had gained 12 per cent market share since launching their app. This definitely had his audience sitting up and taking notice. Generally, people can be scared of change. If you can show where it has been successful before, it helps persuade them. You can spread your parallels to different countries or different industries.

Sometimes negative examples can be equally persuasive (i.e. What will happen if we don't do something?

James also said, "If we don't digitalise, and we continue losing foot fall in our stores, the business won't be viable in less than a year from now." Another sit up and listen moment!

So, now you have all the tips to ace your presentations and the impact of what you are saying: You will have a well-focused presentation with your key message of eight words or less; it's well-structured with your three key areas; you have used parallels to persuade, and proper nouns to hold people's attention, and each time you make a point, it's succinct and memorable, because you have illustrated it.

If you are new to a role or are struggling to think of examples, perhaps show your template to someone else. Brief them on your audience, message, and structure (This is critical, and hopefully you realise this by now.), and ask them if they can think of any examples or points you have left out, or perhaps share some good examples from before you started.

Alternatively, leave it alone, stop thinking about it, and come back to it; your subconscious will start working on it, and you'll think of a great example whilst showering or brushing your teeth!

Get Your Presence Felt

So, how do you get your presence felt? Firstly, how would you describe someone with presence? It can be their build, their reputation, their stage presence, or maybe their body language, or something that they have that you can't quite put your finger on.

One of the things I have observed and studied is that people with presence rarely rush things. They seem relaxed, in control, and confident. Why do I mention presence now, after you know how to nail your presentation content-wise? Because, we are going to work on your openings and conclusions, and it is non-negotiable that you get your presence felt in both of these if you are going to truly elevate your impact.

Most people do not use their openings effectively; they literally say their name as fast as possible, ignore any eye contact, look at their notes or slides, and get through the presentation as quick as possible.

A great presenter wants to get through to the audience, not to the end!

Let me repeat that. Read it slower this time, and pause for 3 seconds when you see ///.

A great presenter /// wants to get through to the audience /// and not /// to the end!

Get it? How often do you see it? Rarely. Sorry, but you'll be an expert observing this now that you know it. You can't not know it. But I don't want you to be an expert observing it. I want you to be an expert delivering it, and for people to describe you as having presence.

Additionally, you sound much more interesting and enthusiastic if you emphasise a few words in each sentence. Try saying the same sentence again out loud, with the pauses, but also emphasising the underlined words. It's a bit like reading a story to a child; you need to act the part. But remember, if you are good at presenting, people assume you are good at your job!

A **great** presenter /// wants to get through to **the audience** /// and **not** /// to the **end**!

You need to give your audience a reason to listen, and distract them from their phones.

You must get your presence felt at the beginning of your presentation and at the end. It's where people remember you. Unfortunately, for most people, they don't settle down till after the opening minute, and they peter out at the end. We need to address this.

So, how do you get your presence felt at the beginning and the end?

Your opening:

Asking a question:

This is particularly good if you are nervous or want to introduce the audience to themselves (i.e. they have a mixed level of knowledge).

Pay attention to the wording of your question so it is easy to understand and answer.

Example: In a presentation about internet retailing, you could ask, "Raise your hand if you have been high street shopping in the last week?"

A startling remark:

Sometimes a startling remark can also work well as an opening. Take some time to research some shocking or surprising statistics that relate to your subject matter.

Example: Sticking to the internet-retailing theme, "Did you know that in 2017, over 6,000 UK high street shops closed their doors, at an average of 16 a day?"

* Source: The Guardian/PricewaterhouseCoopers

Sign posting:

If you have a tendency to go off track, a great tip is to sign post your presentation.

Tell them what you are going to tell them (in your opening) tell them (in your main bit); and tell them what you have told them (in your conclusion). This method keeps you and your audience on track.

It also often prevents unnecessary interruptions and questions, as people know where you are going with the presentation.

Humour:

Using humour is also a good way to start. Some people prefer it; others stay away from it.

I recommend that my clients use it if they are nervous or are presenting in the evening.

There are, however, a few tips to ensure that your humour works.

Firstly, get them laughing early—within the first 25 seconds of starting. The mistake most people make is that they leave it too late. A typical example is a best man's speech.

They get up with a serious look on their face, and then, two or three minutes into it, they put a funny in; but it's too late—no one is set up for humour.

My second tip is to make sure it's apt for your audience. Far too many senior executives put their favourite golf story in, which is inappropriate unless you are at the golf club! Run your joke past someone to test it. What you and I laugh at will make audiences laugh out loud—then there's a magnification element at work.

Thirdly, get the wording right! We have all messed up the punchline of a joke. Write it down and learn it!

When you follow these tips, you will successfully deliver humour, and your audience will laugh. When you get that reaction, it's instant relaxation for you presenting, and instant *connecticating* to you for the audience.

International humour can be more difficult. You need to red light it—gauge the audience, the culture, and the occasion.

One example I have used when speaking abroad, which always gets a laugh, is: What do you call someone who speaks many languages? Multi-lingual

What do you call someone who speaks two languages? Bi-lingual

What do you call someone who speaks one language? English

Apologies if you have heard that one before!

Whichever way you choose to open, it is essential to hit the ground running—don't give your audience an opportunity to drift into passive mode.

The best tip I can give you about openings is to learn them off by heart so that you get your presence felt. If you hear yourself start well, your confidence soars. Conversely, the opposite is true.

It is crucial to practise your opening out loud—I said OUT LOUD!

I always ask my clients if they have practised their opening before they run an upcoming presentation past me, and they usually say, "Yes; on the train, on the way in this morning."

This is in their heads and does not count. You must say it out loud, with emphasis and pauses. You need to sound enthusiastic about it too. The only thing more contagious than enthusiasm is the lack of it. Clients often say, "It's a dry subject." My reply: "No such thing— only a dry presenter." If you are not enthusiastic, no one else will be.

I find it ironic that people can read a child a bedtime story, and make it interesting—but to a board of directors, they put them to sleep. If only it were that easy with children!

So, remember: Learn your openings off by heart, and get your presence felt.

Your Conclusion:

Equally important is how you end. Make your conclusions punchy and abrupt. Don't drag them out. If you say you are concluding, then PLEASE do. Audiences' ears prick up at the mention of conclusion, and they pay particular attention to it, so make it worth their while so that they remember you! So, if you are following the sign posting technique, tell them what you have told them by repeating your message and structure. You need to say it with conviction and to sound like you are ending—make it strong.

"In conclusion, I have presented my structure for success.

Remember: one team, one plan, one goal."

That's it—you need no more! Punchy and abrupt is good.

Sometimes – not always—dramatising your conclusion works.

If we don't do this, our competitors will (and you could slam your hand down firmly on the table as you say this).

A triad can also be effective as a conclusion. This is where three words or phrases are strung together for impact: "Location, location, location," or, "'Innovation built this company; innovation is this company; and innovation is the future for this company."

They are very impactful for conclusions, and leave a lasting impression. A word of caution though: Triads can be overused. Politicians sometimes do this at election time.

So now, go away and prepare a five-minute presentation, using the techniques you have learnt so far.

How long do you think it will take you?

I'll give you a clue.

President Roosevelt was once asked by a journalist how long he spent on a five-minute speech.

He replied: "A good couple of hours."

The journalist was astounded.

"A good couple of hours of presidential time on a five-minute speech—how long do you spend on an hour's speech?"

President Roosevelt: "I am ready now—what's the subject?"

It is a rare art to get your message across in five minutes. Taking something complicated and explaining it in five minutes, while making it relevant to your audience, is the first 'W' in having the WOW factor.

W – What's your message?

Presenting is your most visible skill. Put into practise what you have learnt, and you will be in this elite top five per cent of presenters. If you are good at presenting—remember—people assume you are good at your job! When you can make your job sound easy, you are on the way to promotion becoming inevitable. People begin to notice you. People remember you. People start talking about you.

When you have the two combined, you have just put your foot firmly on the first invisible rung of the ladder gap I spoke about in Chapter 1.

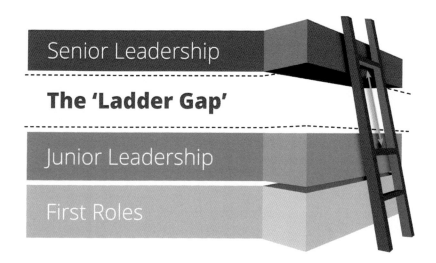

Handling Nerves

Another important aspect of increasing your impact is knowing how to control your nerves. I worry about people who say they don't feel nervous about presenting. They can often come across slightly blasé. Nerves are good and natural; like an athlete, that adrenaline rush can boost your performance. What makes you feel nervous? Often, it is the thought of messing it up, which is a good sign. It means you care and want to get it right. Delivering a presentation is one of the top fears people have. It's because standing (or sitting) in front of a group of people, whilst presenting to them, provokes a flight or fight response. For a nanosecond, your brain is working out whether you will die or not! It's the caveman instinct: Do I fight this animal, or do I chase it and kill it for food? The physiological changes we experience when we are nervous are the same ones the caveman felt. The difference is, doing our presentation is not a life or death situation, despite the fact that it may feel that way sometimes!

Recognise that because of this, it is adrenaline, not nerves, that is making you feel the way you do: Maybe your breathing quickens, your palms feel sweaty, or you get butterflies in your stomach.

I love the phrase: "You can't get rid of butterflies entirely, but you can get them to fly in formation."

It epitomises the essence of you controlling the nerves (the adrenaline), and not the nerves controlling you. Bearing in mind that it is adrenaline causing you to feel this way, you may feel what we associate with nervousness just before you begin. This is because you are sitting still, and the only muscle working is your heart, which is why you can feel it pumping a little more strongly than usual.

You need to give the adrenaline somewhere else to go.

If you have arm rests on your seat, try lifting your body weight with your arms, and changing your position, lifting your bottom off the seat, so your arms take the weight of your body.

As you sit back down into the seat, your heart will be pumping slightly slower—I have tested this out with a heart monitor.

Or (and you can try this now) put both feet flat on the floor. Lift your toes to the ceiling or the sky, keeping your heels on the floor. Can you feel your hamstring stretching? Put your toes back down an up again. Repeat. Again, this gives the adrenaline somewhere else to go. This is a technique like the one taught to actors who have stage fright. Do you know that wobbly, jelly-leg feeling, when you must walk up to the front and start your session? Actors are trained to wriggle their toes inside their shoes, or rock forward and backward very slightly. It's called grounding, and it allows you to feel the ground beneath you, and to reconnect with it when your legs feel like they don't belong to you.

Some of the best presenters I know go for a brisk walk before they present.

If I am speaking at an event, organisers always save me a seat at the front. I stand at the back so that as I am introduced, I walk to the stage to get rid of my adrenaline. These are simple techniques that really work; please try them—I guarantee one of them will work for you.

If you feel less nervous, you'll look more confident and have more impact than most.

Another tip for calming your nerves is to practise, practise, and practise again. However uncomfortable it feels, it is better to feel uncertain when you're practising than when you're delivering for real.

It's equally important to get all of this into perspective.

If your next presentation is a disaster, or you get a standing ovation, you will remember neither of them on your deathbed.

Laughter, family, and memories are much more important. So be positive from now on about presenting.

Most people don't know these tips. Picture someone shaking your hand and saying that it was the best presentation you've ever done. Visualisation is a powerful technique, and it is used by sports psychologists to train top athletes. Eradicate the negative image of you fluffing your lines or clamming up, and replace this with positive visualisation. Picture yourself delivering the most amazing, impactful presentation, with a clear and concise message.

One of the best ways to look natural is to think of something funny or that makes you laugh, just before you start, so that the first thing your audience sees is someone smiling, who looks fun and easy to connect with. In this world of mobile phones, we must remember we need to work harder to get your audience's attention. We are wired to connect through our eyes and not a screen. They will smile back at you, and this is the earliest opportunity for you to get a reaction from your audience. Anything is better than a sea of blank faces staring at you. If you are worried about this, practise it in a mirror—not a McDonald's "have a nice day" smile, but a real, genuine one, coming from a happy memory.

A great tip to relax you (at any time) is to take a slow, deep breath in (count to nine), and then breathe out fully and slowly (count to nine). This calms you down and gets your breathing down into your diaphragm where it needs to be in order to project your voice.

I often have to coach people to get this right. You can feel and see if their voice is coming from their throat. They'll notice it too if they get breathless or suddenly have to stop.

You really lack presence when you do this.

Another side effect of not breathing correctly is something you may notice in other people, or suffer from yourself: a red flush or rash around the neck and chest area. It's caused by a build-up of heat, causing blood vessels to dilate and the blood to flow closer to the skin's surface. Breathing in the way I have explained calms the nerves, helps control the adrenaline, and in turn reduces the likelihood of this happening.

So, relax, breathe slowly, be positive, and smile.

Body Language

As well as a smile (except if you are about to lay off a group of people!), eye contact is another way of getting your presence felt.

Eye contact with your audience is essential throughout your presentation.

The rule of thumb for eye contact is three seconds of good, direct eye contact with someone.

To show you how effective this is, imagine a table with ten people sitting round it.

Within half a minute, you will have good, direct eye contact with them all.

Some people find this a challenge, so do practise it, even while sitting in a room of ten people when you are not speaking. Choose someone, and then count one, two, three, and move on. Eye contact is important, and you may need to get used to it. Some families hardly ever have much eye contact, and this, therefore, needs a lot of effort before it feels natural. If you have a large audience, obviously you cannot do this, but what you can do is grid the audience.

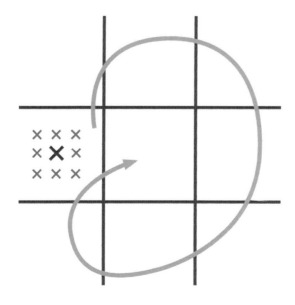

They do not realise you are looking at them, as it could be anyone around the room.

Move your way round the grid, spending three seconds in each bit.

If lights are shining on the audience or you, still do the same. They can still see you!

I have been asked numerous times by clients what they should do with their hands.

Your hands tend to go back to where they started. For example, if you start with your hands on the lectern, they are unlikely to move. My pet hate is people that click pens in their hands! If you start with a pen in your hand and put it down, invariably you will pick it up again. Likewise, if you start with your hands in your pockets or by your side, it becomes difficult to move them once you start. The tip to avoid this is to move them in the beginning - from waist level. Perhaps say good morning or good afternoon, and move your hands outwards as you say it.

If you put yourself into the presentation 100 per cent in terms of delivery, your hands will move naturally.

It is only when people are not listening to you that they notice what you are doing with your hands or anything else distracting. If they are listening to you because you have good impact and are landing your message, you will be in the top five per cent of presenters.

You will now have a template for every presentation you make, and this will help you feel much more confident. If you are fluent with the content of your presentation, your template may be sufficient, especially if it is a more informal presentation. If you prefer more preparation, you could write out the presentation in full, practise it in advance, and on the day, just have the template to prompt you.

For those of you that prefer a checklist, here's our Ten Box Tick sheet.

1. Audience	☐	**6.** Points	☐
2. Purpose	☐	**7.** Examples	☐
3. Message	☐	**8.** Proper Nouns & Parallels	☐
4. Structure/Brainstorm	☐	**9.** Introduction	☐
5. Timings	☐	**10.** Conclusion	☐

Either way, find something that works for you so that you are not reading it.

Now, you may be shouting, "I'll have my slides!" But we have not talked about visual aids.

Visual aids should visually aid YOUR AUDIENCE, and not you!

Work on your presentation, without any! Yes, you heard correctly. And only when you get to the end of filling in your template, ask yourself: Where do visuals make my presentation better for my audience? Do they increase or decrease my impact?

I am not against them in the slightest. As I said earlier, they have their uses. They are great for pictures, graphs, business models, organisational charts, and many more visual things. They are not that good with a lot of words—that is, when they are aiding the presenter and not the audience. As a presenter, you should not speak and look at your slides—that's what pauses are for.

Talking of pauses, you will remember when we were talking about your opening, I said that most people want to get to the end, but a great speaker wants to get through to the audience. We are going to revisit that thought now.

A speaker/presenter, with the WOW factor, is comfortable with silence—the symbol of presence.

Most people fill gaps with unnecessary sounds or words, such as um, so, okay, or right; I even once had a client from Ulster Bank who said, "Now, what do you call it," 18 times in a 14-minute presentation, and had no idea he had said it until I pointed it out and showed him a recording—tough Tara love!

So, how do you get comfortable with pauses?

Let me give you some bad news first: Only 30 per cent of the success of your presentation is down to the content. So, if you get everything right that I've covered so far, and learn it, it's just 3/10 for you.

Seventy per cent of the success of your presentation is HOW you say it.

The good news is that you should be feeling much more confident about your presentation by now. If you have read this far, I know you are serious, not just about getting into the top five per cent of presenters, but you are also seriously committed to elevating your impact, influence, and career, and you want to have the elusive leadership WOW factor.

What I need you to do now is read the two exercises below, out loud somewhere—you'll need five minutes to do it.

So, please come back when you can do this. Do not read on. Please, I mean it.

Go on; get a coffee, check your emails, send a text that puts a smile on your face—GO AWAY.

This will only work if you read this out loud. If you are reading it in your head, you are not taking this seriously, and there is no point reading further. Give the book to someone whose career you want to help and is serious. The only way you can continue without reading this out loud is if you are following our online WOW Your Presentations course, as you will have already submitted a recording of your voice and will have received bespoke impact coaching.

Well done, all the rest of you that are waiting patiently and are serious about elevating your impact.

Read this out loud and record yourself.

Learning a foreign language comes naturally to some people.
But others find it a real struggle. Why is this?
There are several factors which inhibit language learning.
The first is simply a lack of confidence.
Many of us are just too afraid to speak up in case we make a fool
of ourselves. The second reason is a lack of motivation.
If you don't actually need another language
if you can survive with English
Then why bother? It's basic laziness.
Thirdly, some people have a natural aptitude for languages,
women more so than men. The Lebanese, Dutch and Scandinavians
often speak several languages fluently. (The Arab races as a whole,
incidentally, seem to find languages relatively easy.)
And finally, the way people are taught has a bearing on how quickly
they pick up a language.

Well done!

This time, *really* emphasise the words that are underlined.

Where you see a /, pause.
/ for a 1-second pause.
// for a 2-second pause
/// for a 3-second, dramatic pause

Now, read this out loud. Record this one as well. If you know or have been told you are soft-spoken, try projecting your voice. Remember to take a few deep breaths in, very slowly, so that when you exhale, your breathing sinks into your diaphragm. Yes, speak after you have exhaled.

Learning a foreign language
comes naturally to some people.
But others find it a real struggle.//

Why is this?///

There are several factors which
inhibit language learning.//

The first is simply a lack of
confidence.//
Many of us are just too afraid
to speak up/in case we make a fool
of ourselves.//

The second reason/is a lack of motivation.///

If you don't actually need another language/
if you can survive with English
Then why bother? It's basic laziness.

Thirdly, some people have a natural
aptitude for languages,
women more so than men.//
The Lebanese, Dutch and Scandinavians
often speak several languages fluently.//
(The Arab races as a whole, incidentally,
seem to find languages relatively easy.)///

And finally, /the way people are
taught has a bearing on how quickly
they pick up a language.///

Now, how did the second one feel?

Play back your recordings. Notice the difference, the pace, the projection, and your enthusiasm.

Think about those people that impressed you in the last 12 months. You will be beginning to sound more like them now. For some of you, the second one will have felt unnatural but sounded better. This is fine. You need to practise so it becomes more natural. For some, it will immediately feel better. As a minimum, you need to write out your openings and conclusions like this, practicing your lines till you know them off by heart and can say it and mean it.

Either way, practise it or run it past someone whose opinion you trust for some feedback.

For really important presentations, people often ask me how long you should practise. As a guideline, it's one hour of practice for every minute of your presentation, if you want to nail it. You may think this is unrealistic, but it is your most visible skill. You really do need to think of practise in terms of hours rather than minutes.

Next Actions

Complete your presentation template.

Your message in 8 words or less

Key area		Key area		Key area	
Points	Examples	Points	Examples	Points	Examples

Further support is available at *leadershipwowfactor.com/ wowyourpresentations.*

Secret 2 - the O in W**O**W

The **O**rbit Effect
Orbit: an area of activity, interest, or influence

Chapter 5

Know Your Stakeholders

"Leadership is influence."
– John Maxwell

Having worked on the first secret of **WOW** (**W**hat's your impact), it's now time to move onto the second secret, **O**—how to *orbit* your messages to elevate your influence.

Remember, great leaders communicate their messages.

Most people, particularly those who are very good at their job, are not great at communicating what fantastic work they have done, and the benefit to their clients and customers, their departments, and their organisation. This is often due to lack of time, or perhaps not wanting to put themselves out of their comfort zone. I often say to my colleagues, **"Don't be selfish; if not you, who?"**

To have more impact and influence, you need to communicate your critical leadership messages: your Pulse (Chapter 3). Your team and YOUR career are depending on you representing them. Continually ask yourself what your message is and who it is that needs to hear it.

Helen, head of Customer Experience in a large global retailer, spoke at a conference of the global CEOs, and proudly reminded them how they had taken the number one position in the market, three months before. However, she was not reminding them—they did not know, because she had not told them.

She told me that she presumed they knew. It was her job! **"Don't be selfish; if not you, who?"**

Being humble is normally a good thing, but the people who communicate their achievements and the benefits to the business to their stakeholders, get noticed and are more likely to be remembered at promotion time.

The definition of orbit is *an area of activity, interest, and influence.*

You need to *actively* spend time and effort to be interesting, and interested to elevate your *influence*. Successful leaders do this, and they make the time to do it as a career priority.

When you are confident about your messages, you will find that conversations with stakeholders are easier, and you are better equipped to make the most out of opportunities.

They will be excited by your vision and be impressed you have a strategy to deliver it.

People remember and can REPEAT your message—the **O**rbit effect!

If your team knows your messages, they can also cascade them to their peer group and their managers.

However, I have never had a client who was orbiting their stakeholders enough.

You can always ask the stakeholders you do connecticate with, if there is anyone else that:

- is worth me talking to
- might be interested
- might support me or that I could support
- could give me a different point of view
- could help with the challenges
- has experienced this before

This is great news for those who are not keen on promoting themselves. You can get others to do it for you.

Stakeholder Orbit Spreadsheet

One of the easiest ways of doing this, and often a focus for my coaching clients, is to identify their Stakeholder Orbit Spreadsheet— a spreadsheet of people, internally and externally, that they can orbit their messages to. It has their name, job title, department/division, why their relationship/role matters to me, and why my relationship/role matters to them.

Include the people you want to or should be influencing—not just now in this role, but in your next role and your role after that.

I also get my clients to RAG their stakeholders.

Red = little or no relationship

Green = good relationship or someone who champions you

Amber = somewhere in the middle, a lukewarm relationship (e.g., someone who you may have worked closely with some time ago/someone you have recently worked well with on a project)

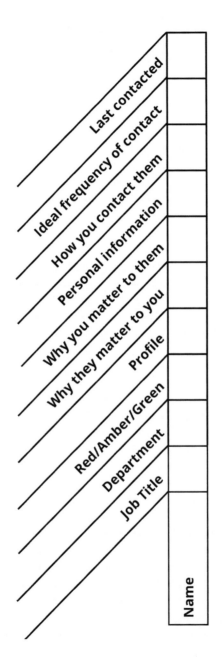

Name	Job Title	Department	Red/Amber/Green	Profile	Why they matter to you	Why you matter to them	Personal information	How you contact them	Ideal frequency of contact	Last contacted

All my clients have been quite blinkered when asked to start working on this and come up with an average of a dozen names. If you are only influencing a dozen people, your impact will be limited.

What you should really be doing as a minimum throughout your career is spending ten per cent of your time—yes, half a day week—nurturing/connecticating these relationships, getting the reds to ambers, the ambers to green, and stopping the greens going to amber or red. Your Stakeholder Orbit Spreadsheet is continually live and continually changing throughout your career, and without activity, it can be a huge career blocker.

Think about: your *past* stakeholders - people you have worked with previously at your current and past jobs; *current* stakeholders internally and externally and *future* stakeholders – who do you want to impact/influence/meet.

Often, because of the ladder gap, people are not balancing their priorities to join future career dots. I often hear clients say, "But my client commitments have been really heavy this month." I always say, "You are YOUR career and YOUR most important client." When that penny drops, and they begin to forward plan their activity—from their Stakeholder Orbit Spreadsheet—they really see their influence and career accelerate.

Internal Stakeholders:

Emma was a driven, talented, and hard-working human resources director for EMEA, for a global facilities management company. Her boss championed her and asked for coaching to elevate her impact and influence.

At the beginning of her coaching programme, I had asked her to start her Stakeholder Orbit Spreadsheet. We discussed her internal stakeholders that she wanted to influence, or those that she should be influencing.

She also spent time thinking about her most important client—her career—and identified that there was an upcoming internal networking opportunity in London that she could attend.

"Who else will be there?" I challenged.

One of them was the CEO from their head office in Chicago.

On the first draft of her stakeholder spreadsheet, he was not listed.

He was on her second!   Most people's first draft of their Stakeholder Orbit Spreadsheet is quite blinkered.

Internally, it's not just your team; it could include: the leadership team, their direct reports, your peers across the business, their direct reports, subsidiary companies, and global colleagues. Widen your thinking. Who will be important to influence, to get promoted, and to get support from now and in the future? Widen your view of who your stakeholders are. Push yourself beyond who you could potentially influence, to possibly, **"Who would it be great to influence?"** Even if it's not in the next few days, what about weeks, months, or years? Time flies, and when these people are in your conscious mind, of who to influence, it is extraordinary what opportunities open up.

I said to her, "If you get the chance to speak to the CEO, what's the one thing you would really like to ask him?" Emma thought for a few seconds, and then declared, "I'd love him to spend a day with my team."

Putting her CEO into her realm of **"Whom would it be great to influence,"** meant she was more likely to take action at building relationships with him.

For Emma, this meant that when she saw him in the bar after the networking event (and after a glass of wine!), she approached him and introduced herself, with her **purpose,** and then courageously said, "I'd love you to spend a day with my team." He replied, "What, do a Richard Branson for the day?" He then joked about how his wife said he should never agree to anything once he'd had a drink.

On my next coaching session, I was excited to hear this update, and that she had met him and asked him. I asked her, "What happened next?" Silence.

She had not taken any more action. "What could you do now to leverage that interaction?"

"Hmm, I could send him an email."

"Go on then," I cajoled.

"What shall I say?"

"What you want and why," I answered.

So, we worked on a very brief email:

Subject: Your Richard Branson Day

Great to meet you last week at the UK networking event. As discussed, I would love you to spend the day with my team. It would show that our company is taking engineering seriously.

I look forward to hearing from you.

Nervously, she pressed send. A few hours later (they are five hours behind!), she got a one-word reply:

"Sure."

Why wouldn't he say yes? It's a no-brainer—and it's an opportunity on his Stakeholder Orbit Spreadsheet of "Whom would it be great to influence?"

His PA was copied in, and they arranged it for eight weeks later, to tie in with his next trip.

When you communicate impactful messages, you make it easy for people to remember you—and not only remember you but talk about you.

When you control the messaging, the cascade effect takes place.

Emma's CEO did spend a day with her team, and after asking herself again, "What can I do now to leverage that interaction?" she hired someone to film the day, and made a great short video of the highlights.

In another coaching session, again taking time to look at her Stakeholder Orbit Spreadsheet, she decided to invite some of her red, amber, and green stakeholders to her upcoming leadership conference. She was clear on her messaging at the conference, *Be Brave*, and managed to incorporate the filming of the CEO's day with her team. The conference was a great success, and six months later, her team won Team of the Year—a great example of the cascade effect.

Not only that, but as winner of the award, she was then invited to Chicago to speak at the head office, bi-annual leadership conference. She was promoted four months later.

External Stakeholders:

Often, external stakeholders can be even more influential in elevating your impact and influence than the people within your organisation. Think of it as what the marketing world refers to as *third party* endorsement; you might not believe an advertisement that sings the praises of a particular product, but if a friend or journalist recommends you try it, it becomes more credible. Your external stakeholders are ideally placed to champion you and give you that third party endorsement, making you and your message infinitely more convincing.

One of my clients, Santosh, now a partner at one of the Big 4 accounting firms, is a perfect example of how external stakeholders can elevate your career to the next level. When I met him for a coffee for the first time, he was a director and a partner promotion candidate.

He was wearing an ill-fitting suit, his eye contact was irregular, and he was fairly soft spoken and humble, and he did not have not much presence. He had been brought up in India by hardworking parents who had saved hard to send him to a good school. He had come to the UK for university, and rose through the ranks to senior manager quickly.

He was hardworking, well respected by those who knew him, and knew his stuff but lacked gravitas, and his profile outside of his own business area was weak.

After a few minutes of conversation, I could tell he was still thinking, feeling, and acting like a senior manager.

Over a course of six coaching sessions taking six months, we worked on his impact, influence, and leadership skills. He worked really hard on his Stakeholder Orbit Spreadsheet, focusing particularly on 20 partners across the firm that he wanted to influence.

Prioritising *know your impact* and *know your stakeholders* is a powerful combination.

His impact and confidence increased dramatically after completing our WOW Your Presentations online course, and he volunteered to contribute his expert knowledge on a bid to win some work with a huge insurance company. The CEO of the insurance company wrote to the partner leading the bid, saying that Santosh's contribution was what secured what went on to become a landmark deal. Santosh asked the partner (at my suggestion) to forward this message to some of the stakeholders on his spreadsheet, to say that if they had any similar requirements, Santosh would be happy to help. He quickly became the go-to person on insurance risk advisory. He also offered to speak to new graduates, and designed and delivered an insurance induction programme for new joiners.

Promotion is inevitable when you are thinking, feeling, acting, and looking like the next level up. Unfortunately, most people think if they show they are working really hard, and arrive first and/or leave last, it means that they are showing commitment; but conversely, this looks like you cannot cope with your workload, and perhaps are struggling with your work- life balance. This is also true of many when they are new to a role and trying to impress. Santosh's experience of achieving partnership in his firm demonstrates how crucial it is to start *being* the level you're striving for, before you even get there.

The same can be said of sending emails way outside of normal business hours. Remember, as a leader, you should be worth following and acting as a visible role model. Exceptions: If your regular hours are arranged so that you can pick up children from school (and your stakeholders are aware of this), you make up the time after your children go to bed.

At one of our sessions, we had worked particularly hard on what kind of attributes Santosh admired in partners, and I had helped him develop those themes. Each day, for a month, he had to text me with something new he was doing, to demonstrate that. This soon became habit. He was feeling like a partner.

We worked on delegating more effectively by developing his number two so that he could spend ten per cent of his time (half a day a week) having stakeholder conversations. I advised him to make the most of this time, particularly with senior business leaders, by asking them about their priorities and challenges.

I then helped Santosh develop articulation of his thoughts, the main issues affecting the firm, and what, as a partner, he thought the firm could do to maximise opportunities and mitigate risks to the business (know your message). He was thinking like a partner.

During a lunch hour on a business trip to Hong Kong, he visited a tailor, and before dinner that night, he collected three very reasonably priced, expensive-looking tailored suits. He was looking like a partner (know your impact).

Over the six months I worked with him, we reflected on his firm's partner attributes, and templated his evidence against them. I encourage people to work on their career template: What evidence do you have at succeeding at this role? What have you learnt from the challenges, and how can you demonstrate you are ready for the next level up?

I got him to do a SWOT exercise on himself. As you may know, SWOT is an acronym for **S**trengths, **W**eaknesses, **O**pportunities, and **T**hreats. It's a strategic management tool taught at most business schools, including Harvard and Stanford, and is used by global companies. It's great to apply to your own leadership development.

Start by listing all your strengths and achievements. Then make a note of your weaknesses and improvement areas needed—include any fears, worries, doubts, and concerns.

What opportunities are there to use your strengths and to overcome your weaknesses? (I don't say weaknesses; it's what you can do better, I say to my clients and my kids!)

Finally, what are the threats (or better still, obstacles!) blocking you now or in the future?

Each time I met Santosh for a coaching session (once a month for half a day), we prioritised his leadership WOW.

What's your impact? Any achievements/challenges/concerns?

Orbit Effect – Whom do I need to influence? Who can help me? Whom can I help?

What's most critical (must do, will do, can do)? How can I leverage this (more of this in Chapters 8, 9, & 10)?

As I mentioned, when I first met Santosh, he was a partner promotion candidate. After all this work developing his impact, influence, and leadership skills, it was then time to work on his presentation to the panel. He needed to focus on his message to them:

Santosh would be the partner to make their firm the *go-to insurance advisory practice.*

He explained this using his three key priorities:

The size of the opportunity to become the *go-to insurance advisory practice.*

How his unique contribution made him the partner to lead this.

His three key priorities as partner to become the *go-to insurance advisory practice.*

I also help my clients navigate the questions they might be asked. For example, "What are your development areas?"

People always ask me: "What's a good one to say for that?"

I bet you can't wait for the answer to that one!

The magic answer is, "The truth." If you don't believe you have a development area, your self-awareness probably needs some attention, and you would benefit from asking and getting some feedback from those around you, about where you might need to improve.

Another question often asked is, "What would it mean to become a director/partner?"

Candidates often answer this in a perfunctory manner: "It's what I have always wanted and worked towards…," etc.

These promotion panels regularly get the same answers from most candidates; you need to be the person who stands out, increasing your impact and giving them something different.

This is where it is critical to *connecticate*.

I asked Santosh, and his first answer followed the perfunctory format. When I delved beyond his humbleness, he told me passionately that it would make his parents' sacrifices (of going without any holidays to send him to boarding school) worthwhile.

That was how he concluded his presentation on why he wanted to be the partner to the *go-to insurance advisory practice.* He was later given feedback that he "kicked the ball right out of the park," and nearly had some of them in tears.

Santosh knew his message, and was his message.

He was successfully promoted and has gone on to lead his firm, becoming the *go-to insurance advisory practice*. He was thinking it, feeling it, and acting it.

Last year, we ran a pilot, Lead with Impact, for Accenture senior managers preparing to become managing directors (MDs). Once I had their names, I asked them what they would like to get from the two days. A few of them mentioned that they would like to hear from some MDs who could share their promotion journey. Thinking about joining their future dots, I asked them, "As a cohort, what MDs would you like to influence?" We invited 5, and two agreed. The senior managers got to meet them and ask questions.

The MDs agreed and shared varied, fascinating, unique stories about their learnings, and about their own career journeys to the top. It was a great session of which both the delegates and the MDs saw the value. Most people are happy to share their experiences—they did not need me to facilitate this. As individuals, or as a cohort, they could have asked the MDs themselves, and leveraged that conversation by showing interest.

One of the top tips shared at the session was that everyone should develop and keep a promotion template, similar to a CV—a one page record of who you are, what your story is, and what your successes have been (pulse your achievements).

Keeping this updated and relevant means that whenever you are asked about your experience, or to take on a new task or position, you are ready with evidence.

One of the attendees, James, put this into action, six weeks later, when another MD asked James what projects he had been working on. Because he had worked on his promotion template, James sounded impressive and interesting, and was able to fully articulate his response. Two months later, the MD needed someone with James' expertise, and asked James' boss if he could have him on secondment for three months.

At the end of his secondment (he worked hard, was clear on his message, and spent half a day a week on his Stakeholder Orbit Spreadsheet, and got a bi-weekly mentor on his main gap), he raised his profile, and people were noticing him, remembering him, and talking about him positively. He was promoted to MD, six months earlier than anticipated—the Orbit Effect again.

It's up to you to create momentum to elevate YOUR impact, influence, and career. Perseverance is key, and success and inevitable promotion belongs to those that take little consistent actions frequently. Try it and see!

RECAP

What's your message, and who needs to hear it?
Whom would it be great to influence?
Prioritise; *know your impact* and *know your stakeholders* is a powerful combination.

Next Action

Start your spreadsheet – whom would it be great to influence?
Who could you speak with to share their career journey?
Prepare your promotion template.
What attributes do you need to be able to demonstrate?
What evidence do you already have?
What could you do to demonstrate that?
What are your gaps?
How can you fill them? Shadow someone/secondment to different business area/internal development/external course/coach/research/read/attend conference?
Who could support/mentor you?
What can you leverage?
What's most critical?
What's your plan?

Chapter 6

Know Your Style

*"Your smile is your logo, your personality is your business card,
how you leave others feeling after having an experience
with you becomes your trademark."*
– Jay Danzie

By now, you will have a good idea about who should appear on your Stakeholder Orbit Spreadsheet (SOS). You will also be thinking more critically about the time and effort it is going to take you to *connecticate* with each individual or group.

With this part of the book focusing on the Orbit effect, an important consideration is that your orbit naturally revolves around *you.* Therefore, in this chapter, the focus is on your style, and how understanding it, and moreover, *adapting* it, is vital if you are going to fully engage with everyone on your SOS.

You don't need to have risen through the ranks in an organisation to appreciate that not everyone you meet in life has the same motivators and responses as yourself; from friends to family members to colleagues and clients, everyone is different, and this can make negotiating relationships challenging at times.

If there is one thing that working with so many different personalities over my career has taught me, it is that I must adapt my own behaviour style to ensure that they truly hear, understand, and engage with my message. This is an area where I have found recognised behaviour profiling models as useful for me as they are for my clients.

There are many behavioural models available on the marketplace, each of which can help us to better understand people's needs, fears, strengths, and weaknesses.

For me, I have found that the most beneficial, over time, is DiSC, developed by psychologist, William Moulton Marston. DiSC is one of the most widely used profiling models in the world; to date, more than two million people have taken the DiSC test. As it was never patented, there are different versions available; however, as a certified Everything DiSC® trainer, that is the one I use. Its value lies in the fact that it focuses on behaviour rather than personality. By definition, behaviour can often encompass a person's skills, abilities, or intelligence, but in the case of DiSC, behaviour is just that: a manner of behaving or acting. As a theory, it's relatable—you don't need an *ology* to understand it—and it offers a common language that people *get* very quickly, whatever their background.

Another beauty of DiSC is that it is non-judgmental; there are no ideal behaviour types—you are the way you are, and there's nothing wrong with that! Its strength is that it encourages you to be more self-aware—and consequently, more aware of the motivations and needs of others—which makes it invaluable in building effective relationships.

This is a crucial point: Your destiny in an organisation is built by your relationships, *not* your abilities.

Talent will get you in the door, but *character* will keep you in the room.

Business strategist, Tony Robbins, a well-recognised authority on the psychology of leadership, is a great exponent of DiSC, praising its use as a tool for self-understanding, saying: "If there is a rare quality in life, it is self-awareness. Self-awareness of the difference between you and your patterns and the impact of your patterns on those around you."

While your natural behaviour will carry you through a lot of the time—and often until you reach a certain point in your career—it is unlikely to be the ideal approach in every situation or with every colleague, particularly when you are looking to make that elusive leap toward the very top of the career ladder. In order to create the Orbit effect, and really give yourself the leadership WOW factor, you need to be *flexible* with your style. Being aware of your style and its impact on others is vital. The good news is, with a bit of effort and empathy, you really can elevate your impact and influence with others.

As DiSC expert, Keith Ayers, says in his book, *Demystifying DiSC*: "There are no good or bad profiles. And no matter what your profile is, there will be times when being yourself will work just fine for you, and there will be times when it doesn't work. At times like this, when being yourself does not produce positive results for you, you need to be able to adapt your thinking and behaviour to be more effective." Whomever you meet, you need to put their hat on. I'm not talking about mirroring here; I simply mean appealing to their drivers and eliminating their fears.

Like other theories, the DiSC model categorises behaviours into four dimensions or behavioural styles: Dominance (D), Influence (I), Steadiness (S) and Conscientiousness (C). Where the theory comes into its own is that it focuses on stimulus and response; so, depending on which dimension a person most identifies with, they will exhibit certain types of actions or reactions when faced with an individual event or set of circumstances.

Take a look at the diagram on page 85. Which dimension best describes you or the people around you? Do you recognise anyone in particular?

In my training courses, I recommend that delegates concentrate on learning 3–5 traits for each of the dimensions—don't be alarmed, I am not asking you to become a DiSC expert! It is fairly simple and quick to spot what *types* people are. Ask yourself these questions:

You can also think about how they greet you. If the first thing they say is, "How can I help you?" it is likely they are a D or a C. If, on the other hand, they greet you with a chat and try to build rapport, they will probably be an I or an S. Try this test on everyone you meet; you will get so good at it that you will have them sussed in the first 30 seconds!

You can try the test for yourself—and get a full analysis of your behavioural style—by visiting www.wiley.com.

The table provides a broad outline of the traits that characterise each of the dimensions, how to adapt your behaviour to *connecticate* with each style, and also the limitations to keep in mind:

When considering different behaviour types, it can be interesting to think about people in public life. Take Donald Trump, a fine example of a core D-type character: assertive, competitive, challenging, and direct. How about his predecessor, Barack Obama? Persuasive, passionate, and people-focused, he is clearly an I-type. Or consider Queen Elizabeth II—reliable, steady, and consistent, but resistant to change—she can only be an S.

While we tend to fit into one dimension, many of us are a blend, and veer slightly into the next quarter, giving us all subtle nuances to our behaviour. So, a Di-type person may be ambitious and results-driven but also persuasive and good at making the connections

Dominance	Influence	Steadiness	Conscientiousness
D	**i**	**S**	**C**
Top traits:			
Driven, competitive, demanding, challenging, forceful, direct, assertive	Enthusiastic, optimistic, persuasive, magnetic, energetic, passionate	Patient, reliable, diligent, team player, predictable, facilitating, consistently high quality output	Accurate, compliant, analytical, perfectionist, detailed, thorough
Motivated by:			
Results, winning, control	Recognition, wanting to be liked, creating a 'perfect world'	Systems, predictability, an easy life	Fear, recognition of expertise and accomplishment, attention to quality
Need to make an effort to:			
Collaborate more Be more humble	Make decisions Be responsive Communicate delivery achievements	Be bold and brave Innovate Be solution focused	Have more empathy Be passionate
How to behave with them:			
Talk about solutions not feelings Keep it short and to the point – top line only Compliment results	Reinforce their contribution on a regular basis Tell them they are making a difference Give them your time – schedule in meetings	Talk slower Build rapport and trust Give them time to think Provide details and reassurances Be there for them	Let them know timescales Get them to verbalise acceptance Give them lots of information Check in with them but at arm's lengths
Limitations:			
Get frustrated, they can talk over people, they can be cutting	Visually emotional Frustration Can explode Go on the attack Worry what people think	Not sharing information Take on too much Take things personally Change resistant	Critical of standards (self and others) Can be seen as lacking creativity

needed to get those results, while a Dc-type is still concerned with results, but is more controlling, demanding facts and details. Conversely, an Si-type person shows great enthusiasm and thrives on collaboration and a positive environment, but requires the support of others, whereas an Sc-type, while also needing support, prefers a calm, stable environment and fixed goals.

Recognising that people are not pure versions of one dimension or another—and communicating with them in terms of their traits—can be powerful; it is key to improving every interaction you have, and will ultimately give you that competitive edge.

As a coach and trainer, I definitely practice what I preach in terms of DiSC, adapting my behaviour to the people I meet, and making sure I put myself in their shoes before starting a conversation. For example, I might be pitching a team-wide presentation skills course to a company CEO. Recognising that she is a D-type person, I will make sure that our conversation is brief and straight to the point. I'll concentrate on telling her how the course will solve the problem of her having to spend hours listening to long and waffling presentations. I'll also focus on the result: that her team will learn how to get their message across clearly and confidently, and be put into the top five per cent of presenters. I may also need to liaise with the HR director, who decides how the company's training budget should be spent. He may be an I-type person, so I would suggest we meet over a coffee for an hour so I can explain the course in a more relaxed environment, giving him my time and attention, and building rapport. When explaining the benefits of the course, I'll be sure to reinforce the fact that it will help him make a real difference to the presentation skills of his staff, and that they will feel much more confident after the training.

I also adopt this flexible approach with my own team, and they with me. My PA is an S-type person, whereas I am a D. Sometimes I will make what I call a D phone call to her, where I literally dump all my action points in rapid-fire. However, I know that on the back of that, I will need to schedule some S time with her, where we go through the diary step-by-step, and compile a list of key action points so she is clear on her priorities. As a team, we also need to make sure we plan some C time, which neither of us enjoy, but which we need to do in order to fine-tune the details of things like business proposals and marketing campaigns. A little give and take, and flexibility, means we function more effectively as a team.

As a coach, I have met many people who clearly need to adapt their behaviour if they are going to make positive changes in their organisation. Take Alan, for example, the MD of a large manufacturing company. Having received pretty negative 360° feedback from the team around him (he was known to destroy people—not the best accolade), I was taken on as a coach to work with him on his leadership style. On entering the room, it took only seconds to realise he was a classic D—authoritative and direct, he pointed his finger at me throughout our conversation.

"Do you realise you are pointing at me while you're talking? It's very intimidating," I said.

He had absolutely no idea he was doing it, and was quite taken aback. If I felt like this as a visitor, was it any surprise that employees were scared to make contributions or mistakes? Having opened his eyes to how he came across to others, we worked on adapting his behaviours to build relationships and get the best out of the people around him.

At the opposing end of the spectrum was Mark, a highly effective and accomplished accountant in a Big Four practice, who struggled to make that all important jump to director level. He had done everything right—worked hard, knew his subject inside out—but something was holding him back from promotion. On meeting him, I knew instantly he was a C. Although excellent at his job, he lacked rapport, shuffling into the room with barely a handshake. He was good at describing his technical accomplishments, but failed to convey what he could achieve for the business. My coaching sessions involved getting him to introduce some D and I traits into his behaviour, with a focus on showing a friendlier demeanour, and communicating the results he had achieved. He soon got the promotion he deserved.

This last story brings me to my next point. While I am clearly an advocate of DiSC and building flexibility into your communication approach, no chapter on developing your style would be complete without also covering likeability and empathy; it may sound obvious, but both are vital to building strong relationships with colleagues, clients, and customers.

While I-types find likeability and empathy more natural, the rest of us need to make more effort to bring these qualities into our everyday interactions. You never know, you may find you enjoy it—at the very least, you will help people feel better about themselves! The motivational speaker, Jay Danzie, summed this up perfectly: *"Your smile is your business card, your personality is your logo, and how you leave others feeling after an experience with you becomes your trademark."*

The power of a smile cannot be underestimated, even when walking down a corridor or from the car park, or greeting receptionists. As a child, I always looked more serious than I was, so I've consciously worked at it, and when I open a door, I pause for a millisecond before I open it, and I make sure I am smiling. Generally, I am now described as friendly.

A point of warning: While it's great to display non-verbal confidence, it is important not to go overboard on the physical signals (remember the pointing MD!); you do not want to come across as self-important and disinterested in others' points of view—no one likes a dictator.

Have you ever heard that the most captivating people in a room are often the best listeners? Boring people tend to drone on and on, without picking up on body language cues telling them people have heard enough. Good listeners don't dominate the conversation, are interested in other people, and ask questions to show respect. Try it out for yourself next time you are at a networking event or meeting a new client: If you learn something about someone, ask them how or why they did it, or what they enjoyed the most about it—people generally love talking about themselves; it's a key bonding experience. Actively respond by showing you are impressed, or by paying them a compliment, and that bond will strengthen more.

Conversely, when you are talking about yourself, don't forget it's OK to be slightly vulnerable, or to admit a failing or weakness; people will respond better to the *authentic* you.

Remember that smile at the beginning? Make sure you end with it too, and combine it with a handshake, telling them how much you enjoyed meeting them.

Lastly, if you have made a good connection with someone, there is no reason why you cannot follow up with a call or email, asking if there is anything you can do to help them, particularly if you want to ask them for something yourself.

Of course, likeability and empathy are not only relevant to situations where you are meeting new people. Getting the leadership WOW factor also relies on building strong relationships within your business with colleagues you see every day. Put people at the heart of everything you do; be mindful of how others might feel, and tailor your responses accordingly. Rather than rushing past a colleague in the corridor, take time to look up, smile, and call them by their name. If you are in a catch-up meeting, ask questions, *listen* to the answers, and acknowledge what their worries or concerns are.

Are They OK?

When projects go well, be sure to let the people involved know; not only with on-the-spot praise, but perhaps an impromptu celebration. Schedule time for non-work related activities too, even if it's a quick lunch (and avoid talking shop). The feeling of trust and empathy that this generates will pay huge dividends, enabling you to truly *connecticate* with each and every stakeholder in your orbit.

Next Actions:

Think about yourself and the people around you – what DiSC category best describes you/them?
Add a Profile column to your Stakeholder Orbit Spreadsheet (SOS) to put their DiSC profile
Be flexible – adapt your behaviour to the people you meet
Focus on developing likeability and empathy – listen, ask questions, put people first
Watch Brené Brown's empathy video on YouTube

Chapter 7

Know Your Influence

"Influence is when you are not the one talking and yet your words fill the room; when you are absent and yet your presence is felt everywhere."
– Temitope Ibrahim

Balconies

Having worked on identifying your stakeholders and how to orbit your message to them to increase your impact, it is worth considering categorising your **balconies** to ensure you elevate your influence in all areas. Your balconies are where you need to step out of your day-to-day thinking and activity, and have some reflection time in the areas (balconies) that are often forgotten and keep you where you are in terms of your career.

The reason I say this is that you should step onto each balcony—metaphorically speaking—and consider what's happening on that balcony, and potentially who you could possibly influence, or who could influence you, and then put them onto your Stakeholder Orbit Spreadsheet (SOS).

Also, it is very important to see things from their view/perspective/balcony—remember Know Your Audience, from Chapter 2, and where possible, think about their style (Chapter 6).

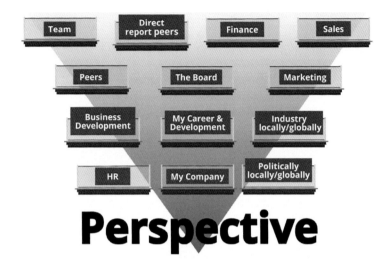

Perspective

You should have all your team as one balcony. As well as the people who work for you, this would also include your boss and administrative assistant.

Other balconies could be your boss's peers, your direct report's peers, the board, finance team, marketing team, digital sales team, business development team, HR, and any others you can think of, including elsewhere in the world if you work for a global company.

Also, it is worth having separate balconies for your industry, your career, and your development.

Your industry balcony will have the movers, shakers, prospective clients, and perhaps even competitors in your industry who you would like to talk to or potentially meet at networking events, or who might hear about you.

Your career balcony could have previous bosses or colleagues whom you may potentially want to recruit or work for. It could include headhunters, who you could work with on your next move.

Your development balcony should have any past, present, or future coaches and mentors, as well as contacts for any potential courses you may want to do, to address your development areas. Internal HR contacts should also be considered here.

I also have a Tara Fennessy PLC balcony. The people on my stakeholder spreadsheet are my speaking guru, who regularly speaks to thousands globally, and always has plenty of experience to share; my marketing guru, who is in a complementary business; my designer guru, who brings my content to life in diagrams; my neuroscience guru, who keeps me up to date with the latest findings; my coaching guru, for supervision; my leadership development guru, with whom I brainstorm innovative leadership development models; my technology guru, who continues to help me with the basics and new apps; and my health and wellbeing guru, who helps me retain balance and look after myself.

I work hard at my relationships, my results, and my reputation, mainly through connecticating regularly with those on my **SOS**—at least 20% of my time—one day a week just on this. It could be by email, text, a call, or a meet up, and it's worth remembering your *last contact* tab on your **SOS** to record this.

One page of your spreadsheet should also be for external stakeholders. These balconies could be: Your Clients, Your Pipeline, Your Targets, Your Competitors.

You cannot underestimate how important this is. YOUR relationships and ability to connecticate are critical if you want to elevate YOUR influence. YOUR ability to listen, ask questions, be interested and interesting in other people's priorities, challenges, challenges, feelings and opinions is critical to broaden your business perspective. YOUR ability to see, discover, and challenge what the landscape looks like to others—internally, in your wider industry and in current affairs—is vital if you want to elevate your impact,

influence, and career. YOUR conversations with stakeholders , your interest in the bigger picture and your ability to contribute in part to the business challenges and priorities are what help you start feeling/thinking/acting/behaving and looking like a leader ready for the next stage in your career. YOUR growth, YOUR development must be owned by YOU!

Knowing your stakeholders' drives, motivations, worries, and concerns is key. Remember the column in your spreadsheet: *What's important to them?* You can find this out by asking them or listening for clues when they talk about themselves or other people. If you need to, ask them some questions or do some research to find out.

What is their wife/partner/ kids' names? Where do they live, and where do they go on holiday? (Remember the proper nouns tips.) What are their hobbies? Sometimes people are reserved about doing this; they fear it might make them appear nosey and intrusive. Please put that reserve to one side and believe that what it really does is show interest in the things that are important to them. If you do this, not only do you seem more interested, but you also seem more caring, and you are likely to build a deeper relationship with your stakeholders. Humans are wired to connect, and we should spend more time talking to a wider range of colleagues about work and not work!

The challenge people find in elevating their influence is that it is often limited. This is because you are more likely to naturally go toward people who are more like you, or with whom you have something in common. These are probably your green stakeholders, or maybe a few ambers. Check and see! As I mentioned in Chapter 6, adapting your style is another critical skill we help our clients with in our training and coaching programmes. We all have a natural style that helps us get so far in life and so far up the corporate ladder. To elevate your career and have influence, you need to adapt that natural way of doing things, and key into other people's styles.

You are probably beginning to think that adapting your style and connecticating with your **SOS** takes time, and you are likely to be wondering how this is possible.

Often, my clients have their balance of time wrong. If you are not doing much of this already, how will you find even more time on top of a heavy workload?

Time Buckets

Let me introduce you to your **Time Buckets**.

Analyse what you spent your time doing last month, and put those activities into your Time Buckets (e.g., 1-1s with team, client updates, pitches for work, compliance meetings, admin, travelling, etc.).

Put a percentage of your total time, and the hours per week/or fortnight/or month that you spent on them. If you do mainly the same things every week, then do it over a week. If a month or four weeks is a better time period to reflect the main things you spend your time doing, then do it over a month. My clients generally have no time for vital activities like strategic thinking, urgent matters that crop up, development time (e.g., conference, coaching, training, reading industry journals), attending networking events, or critically, stakeholder time. They also get slightly or very startled at where their time has been spent.

Often, they are also working too many hours.

As I mentioned earlier, a common reason why people are not promoted is that they do not look to be coping well with their workload. I have spent many hours interviewing senior executives about why they promote and why they don't. The ladder gap mentality usually means that working really hard and putting in long hours has got you to a certain level, but it often keeps you stuck there.

	month 1	month 6
Team 1-1's	25%	10%
SOS 1-1's	5%	12.5%
Client updates	10%	10%
Developing Pipeline	10%	17.5%
Admin	25%	13%
Breaks	5%	5%
Career development	0%	5%
Reflection/Strategy time	0%	5%
Team meetings	20%	15%
Compliance/Quality Meetings	5%	5%
Networking	0%	12%

Not prioritising your family time or wellbeing is often seen as detrimental to career progression at the higher levels.

So now, let's do the Time Bucket exercise again, but instead, think about where you would like it to be six months from now—potentially working a shorter week and getting better balance of your time?

It's now worth strategising what you will work on each month, from now until then, to get you there.

Perhaps a big project finishes soon. Perhaps you should be delegating more, but initially you may need to spend a bit of extra time coaching your direct reports. Could some meetings be shorter or less frequent? Could you work from home to get your admin done or focus on your strategy work? Could you achieve more when you travel? For example, get the train instead of driving, or do something that you need to concentrate on whilst on a long-haul plane journey. I do some of my best work then—no phones, no interruptions—and that's where I scope out my thoughts for a new article, course, or brochure. What questions do you need to ask yourself or others about what's possible?

I was coaching three emerging leaders of a company, separately, and realised they spent a lot of time in their cars driving to see clients, as they each had a large region to cover. When you added up their travelling time, it was 20 days travelling between them per month. I suggested they ask their CEO if they could get a company chauffer for six days every month, so that for two days each month, they would be able to do prep work whilst travelling, FaceTime team members, and work shorter hours. Their productivity, wellbeing, and effectiveness improved dramatically in a month, and the company saved money! Look at the bigger picture to see what's possible, and this could help you to perform at your best!

Working on improving the balance of your time can help you feel less overwhelmed and look more in control.

Show your PA or your team what you are trying to achieve so they can help you, perhaps by interrupting less or not contacting you when you are working from home. Maybe say no to things, or spend more time on your development or with people you need to influence.

Perhaps two hours extra time rehearsing important presentations this month means more chance of winning a bigger contract, which results in less time on business development and admin, six months down the line.

Don't have 30 or 60-minute meetings; instead, make them a maximum of 20 or 45 minutes, or even shorter where possible.

Review last week's diary, and identify all the things that took longer than they needed to.

Are your emails punchy and clear, or is there a long chain of messages on a certain issue?

Spending a little extra time on your emails, asking yourself what your message is (in header), and what your structure is (three areas of attention), as well as being clear on your points and examples, can save a lot of time for you and others in the long run.

Make sure every single one of your communications ends with a *Call to Action*.

If you can't think what action you want someone to take as a result of a communication, seriously consider not sending it.

Start your prep with the call to action: What do you want them to do after they have heard/read this?

Then create a shorter communication focused on only getting them to DO—think less background, more direction.

Alternatively, stop emailing, and pick up the phone! Conversations solve issues faster than criticism and blame.

Come out of cc'd emails; tell the sender that you don't read them, and that you trust them, or just get them to let you know if there's an issue.

Decline meetings you don't need to go to, or ask yourself if someone else could go.

Identify which of these will save you the most time and will be really easy to do.

Apply this as a target for this next month. Each month, aim to work 20 per cent toward your six-month target.

It won't work like a military operation every month, but it should make you much more aware of how you spend your time, and help you to prioritise, making you more effective. Within three months, you'll feel a difference; and in six months, you'll be amazed at the contrast and impact you have made on your leadership WOW factor.

No chapter on influence would be complete without looking at your online presence, as increasingly, the internet has become people's first point of contact with you.

If people are beginning to hear your name from the Orbit effect, for the right reasons, they are likely to check you out via your company website or social media channels before they get in touch.

In terms of your online presence, it's worth thinking about or talking to clients or colleagues about the best platforms to increase your impact and influence.

Do/can you say anything about breaking news on Twitter, or post some interesting pictures of products or team activities on Instagram?

Does/should your company use Facebook? It's worth researching whether it's the right channel for reaching your particular market/audience.

Do your contacts/potential clients/SOS contacts use it?

Remember that what you do this week will help build a credible online presence in the future. LinkedIn has more than 500 million users, 40 per cent of whom check in daily. LinkedIn is becoming more interactive, giving users the ability to post rich media, like videos and images. Yesterday is now your digital history. Did you have any impact or influence?

I check out most people I am about to meet (not least so that I can recognise them at reception), or hear about on LinkedIn. First impressions count, as we all know, yet I am amazed at the profile photos people use—and some don't even have any. Nine out of ten are unprofessional for various reasons (e.g., wearing sunglasses, looking scruffy, out of focus, poor angle, or not up to date, and looking nothing like them).

Because of that, the good news is that a photo of you smiling and looking professional, whilst capturing your personality, helps you have the WOW factor. If you are looking to change jobs, I would recommend investing in a professional headshot.

Profiles with photos get seven times as many views as profiles without them.

Update your status to show that you are engaging with others and are up to date. It can be of an event you are at (if you are presenting, post a photo or video if permissible), an upgrade in your job skills, a photo of your team event, or maybe bragging a little about an achievement or award you have won, or share another post or article that you are mentioned in. You can also share your slides from a presentation. You can connecticate with people by mentioning them too. Simply type in the @ symbol, followed by their name. Often, those mentioned will like or comment or share. This helps you have more impact and more reach, as your post will be seen by their connections.

Perhaps someone on your SOS that you want to meet is a contact of someone you are connected with (which means they are your second contact). This makes it easy for them to say yes to a connection request from you. Alternatively, you might want to ask your contact to introduce you first. LinkedIn recommends that you have at least 50 people on your network.

If you have an email address, you can send a connection request. Connect with current colleagues, past colleagues, friends, and customers. It's often great to re-connect with someone you have not seen for a while, either personally or professionally—don't forget that we are wired to connect. Ideally, don't use the default connection request. Give them a reason to connect, **with a personalised invite**. For example:

"We keep running into each other; I thought it would be great to connect here."

"Hi; hope all is well with you. How's everything going?"

"Sean suggested we connect, if you are happy to."

I have connected with past delegates from courses that I have been on and companies that I have left.

You can also endorse people very easily. You can thank people for endorsements, but it is not always necessary. If people give you recommendations, I would make a point of thanking them, as it takes effort. If a happy client, at the end of a project, asks if there is anything he can do to let people know what a good job you have done, you could suggest a recommendation. Remember that what you do this week joins future career dots!

The LinkedIn desktop version has the most features, but the mobile app is great too.

It's also really good to see what your contacts are up to—keep a limit on how much time you spend though!

Start by liking posts, then commenting, then sharing and then contributing. Being active once a week for a month doing each of these means in 4 months you will have raised your profile and your influence. Keep it up though so you are front of mind for potential contacts and become a thought leader in your area.

You can also get the premium service (at a cost) with it, which enables you to see when people have changed jobs—another reason to get in contact. You can suggest meeting for a coffee, for breakfast or lunch, or for a drink if you want to as well.

Premium also means that you can use privacy settings so that people don't know you are looking at their profiles.

It is a good idea to keep your profile up to date by going to settings (e.g., Edit Public Profile, and adding company website). Take a look at what else you can do. LinkedIn helps you complete your profile and to wow your summary, and maybe some of your PULSE would be useful. People will then begin to get an idea of your personality (yes, that's a good thing).

Even filling in your old school helps you connecticate (although, remember to turn off *activity broadcast*, so LinkedIn doesn't send announcements to everyone each time you edit your profile). Listing hobbies and volunteer work is important for people who want to connect with you. I know it may not seem relevant, but you never know what people are looking for, or how much easier it is if you have things in common with people.

There are many useful groups on LinkedIn, to which you can send a request to join. This demonstrates that you are interested and engaged with a particular topic or sector, and helps you keep up to date. More importantly, you get noticed when you engage with groups. You can watch conversations for a while to see how people relate to each other if you are not confident. When you are ready, you could even consider starting your own group.

What else can you do to raise your profile?

Raising your corporate profile does not necessarily have to revolve around your specific role. Other activities—both corporate and non-work related—can also play a huge part, helping to get your personality across, and showcasing what you are like to work with.

Clients of mine have done various things, such as:

- Writing monthly newsletters, and getting others to contribute.
- Setting a successful Guinness World Record.
- Hiring a *pudding stop'* van to come to the office for the afternoon (a great hit).
- Organising charity functions and inviting local press.

One did a video diary of *A Day in the Life of....* (It was so successful that he followed it up with *A Week in the Life of...*, which became so popular that it became a monthly event, with different people in it.)

Ask yourself:

What more can you do for the benefit of your team, your business, your community, and your hobbies?

What is your contribution personally to make work more fun, exciting, and interesting?

Introducing an element of fun into the workplace reduces stress levels, increases trust and collaboration, and generally makes us all happier.

What is your contribution at work? Maybe look at the person whose job you want, or who has a similar job to you—do they contribute more?

Could you mentor someone or even a few people?

Could you volunteer to present/speak to graduates/a new starter, to tell them about what you do or to introduce them to the company?

Keep going—what more could you do?

Perhaps you could do the milk round at universities, promoting your company to potential postgraduates.

Or could you contribute to some thought leadership, within your industry, on a new blueprint for success/business model, based on a project you have completed, or share your learnings from something that did not go well, so that no one else makes that mistake?

Could you invite someone externally, or perhaps someone from head office, to speak to your team or cohort?

Who is in your network that you could get to come in and disrupt your company's thinking in an area?

Who could you collaborate with to have more influence? Someone in another department?

Could you get together some of the experts in your firm, to articulate their thoughts about future trends, and then invite a group of potentially interested clients to a breakfast meeting to share them?

One of my UK clients at Accenture did just this. Gary invited some of the big banks' chief technology officers to discuss future trends in the banking sector, as well as the most senior person from Accenture USA to virtually join them to share his views. The result was elevated impact with all his senior colleagues, and more influence with his potential customers. (In fact, three months later, he won a £10m contract from one of them, and was promoted.)

He also felt much more confident about the Orbit effect, and now coaches his team members. So many people want to work in their team now; they don't have to recruit, and they have a waiting list internally! I love the fact that the legacy of our training and coaching is that people don't need us again.

Because we make it simple, practical, relatable, and instantly applicable, they become expert at it themselves very quickly.

If you are not sure where you can add greater influence, ask yourself some more questions:

- What do other people say you are good at?
- What do people ask for your help on?
- How can you leverage that knowledge?

One of my clients had OCD, and he presented to his board on how it was a strength when applied to certain areas of the business. He suggested that he lead development in these areas. They said yes, and he cut out a new role for himself, and a bigger salary!

What is possible? Make a suggestion. The worst-case scenario is that they say no; although in my experience, people generally say yes to these suggestions because they are rarely offered.

What about your development areas? How can you further elevate your influence?

Remember Emma from JLL? One of her development areas was marketing. During my coaching programme with her, we discussed how she would remain open to possibilities of narrowing this gap.

Coincidentally, a few months later, the marketing director resigned, and the new one recruited could not start for three months. Emma and I discussed the possibility of her working as acting marketing director.

There were challenges that worried her: How would she find the time? Was she able enough?

I asked how good the marketing department was, and she said they were excellent and that she probably would just need to be there if there were any problems. So, realistically, it would require only 10 per cent of her time.

I asked who her marketing guru was on Emma PLC, and she said that it was the global marketing director in their Chicago head office (who she had met when she spoke there). She checked with him, and he agreed that he would support her should she be challenged by anything she could not handle. It was a stretch, yes, but she was up for it, and ambitious, and said yes. She did a great job—the marketing team loved her leadership style and her challenges. Emma learnt loads about marketing, and developed her presentations externally and internally—she was being invited and was volunteering regularly in her normal role, and the marketing team helped wow her slides with great videos. It was a win for Emma, a win for the team, and a win for the business. She was promoted again—twice in 18 months.

A little bit of action can (and usually does) have a big impact on your influence.

We ran a Shape a Team Extraordinaire' team event for a marketing department of one of the UK's leading food brands.

Marketeers tend to be I-types (Influence types). Knowing this, I anticipated that they would have loads of fantastic, creative ideas of how to *put more (of their) bakery products in every shopping basket*— their Purpose.

To disrupt their 'I' brains so they could use all their experience and knowledge, I asked, "If you could only do one, what would that be?"

They said that they would put all their marketing budget on one TV commercial, with someone famous endorsing their product.

We worked on them presenting that idea to the board, who were very impressed and said yes. The TV advert became a Christmas hit, and they had their sales hit record levels. In fact, retailers, who had previously not stocked their products, rang them up to ask how quickly they could get them in!

Be open to what's possible.

People often ask me what my best coaching tip is.

My answer, for teams and individuals, is always: "Ask a great question'!"

The better the question, the more powerful the answer, and unlike many other coaches, I don't have a list. Laser focused listening—knowing my audience (and their profile)—means that I intuitively know what questions to ask.

I often coach people in their first six months of a new role, and always have a session before they start. **"What sort of impact do you want to have when you land?"** is definitely a good question to think about and decide on.

A client of mine, Martin, wanted to be friendly and professional, as his predecessor was not very popular.

After the announcement that he would be starting, he was pleased to receive LinkedIn connection requests from his future colleagues.

"So, did you accept them?" I asked. "Of course," he said.

"And what friendly and professional reply did you send back?" "Hmmm," was his response.

I have a phrase, which you will see as some of the chapter titles in this book: "Know your message; be your message." It's even on my business cards.

Identifying what messages you want to be giving out has a lot more power when you live and breathe them day to day. Martin had a great opportunity to have friendly and professional impact before he started.

A week before he started, he also showed me an email he had drafted, which he was planning to send out on his first day. I challenged him on how friendly and professional an email was on his first day.

"Hmm, good point."

Instead, he decided to record a five-minute video at home, saying a bit about himself, and getting his kids to say a quick hi. He said that his plan was to get around to the three sites, in the first three weeks, to meet them all.

The HR director told him a month later that his initial impact was the best she had ever seen, and she literally used the words, *friendly and professional*, without her having known his plan.

Know your message; be your message!

Working hard to increase your influence takes time and effort, but it's worth it. I am a great believer in recognising and celebrating achievements and success with others, but also with yourself. When you know something is working, and you have achieved, it is worth giving yourself that recognition too.

My vision, as I have mentioned, is to be *Best Bespoke Global Leadership Training & Coaching Experience* , and in 2011, I was working with clients in Hong Kong. I was with my last client before heading to the airport, and I was looking forward to my return home. The impact of that trip suddenly dawned on me—that I had just made a significant step towards that vision—I was working in Hong Kong, and I had gone global! At the airport, I bought myself a watch that I'd always wanted. I still wear it now, and every time I look at it, it's a celebration of my milestone, and a recognition of success. I already have my eye on a Tiffany ring for when this book gets published!

Your Next Actions

Write out your balconies.

Are all your internal and external balconies identified on your SOS Stakeholder Orbit Spreadsheet? Are you Linkedin with them?

What are the opportunities you can create to connecticate with your stakeholders?

What can you do to leverage your interactions?

Analyse your current time buckets.

Do time buckets again for how you would like it to be in six months (Each month, plan to increase 15–20 per cent toward your six-month target on each of your buckets).

Chapter 8

Know Your Team

"Outstanding leaders go the extra mile to boost their people's self-esteem.If people believe in themselves, it's amazing what they can accomplish."
– Sam Walton

I agree with this quote—but your leadership WOW factor goes a step further.

If you can boost your team's belief and esteem, they can accomplish great things.

Knowing your team is Step 1.

Attracting great people, and getting them to glue together (even if just for a project), is critical for leaders today.

When a leader and team are clear on their vision and their strategy to get there, they accelerate faster toward their goal. It's also much easier to recruit, attract, and retain people.

Nowadays, I am being called into businesses much more to help teams improve the way they work.

I believe that the key for business success, going forward, is when teams lead the way and show the way.

In our Shape a Team Extraordinaire workshop, I say that *"the team that rewires, inspires."*

A team's success in today's age can be measured by their team culture, how quickly they can adapt, and how they communicate with each other.

As a leader, you must align people, not just to your vision, but more importantly, to their own team vision and how they will all get there. A powerful tool for a team's success is to do a Team Pulse.

I facilitated the UK's leading Bakery insight team to create their Team Pulse. They asked me to work with them, as they had a lot of ideas to shape the business but were not managing to influence the board. This is what emerged from our sessions:

Purpose – What is it you really do?
Inspire sustainable growth through shopper and consumer insight.

Uniqueness – How are you as a team, uniquely placed to deliver that purpose?
We understand the shopper journey from every angle.

Leadership – What is your team's leadership vision?
More bakery in every basket (which was their company's vision).

What's your team strategy for more bakery in every basket?
A win for shoppers, win for retailers, and a win for us.

What will your team legacy be?
Be the heartbeat for strategic decision-making.

Knowing their PULSE messages really re-wired their energy and their contribution to the business.

When they came up with their uniqueness, it was a powerful moment, and their confidence really shot up when they realised they were the only team that understood the shopper journey from every angle.

Doing their team PULSE really helped them articulate their critical leadership messages to influence the board. They also leveraged their team pulse in all their presentations, conversations, phone calls, and even emails. This consistency of their message was cascaded throughout the organisation, which helped to elevate their presence and profile, and contributed hugely to the company's business goals. They were able to collectively focus on their results and stay continuously committed and supportive of each other.

Some follow-up work with me, on how to wow their presentations to the board, helped them influence strategic decision-making going forward.

When your team champions excellence in the business, their *best practice* becomes *common practice*, which contributes to your team legacy.

Focus on collective results. Do not underestimate how much your PULSE messages matter.

Inspire them with compelling and clear messages.

Our Shape a Team Extraordinaire workshop shows the teams we work with how to find and unleash their WOW factor. There are 5 cornerstones that help teams become courageous, collaborative, and confident.

B rave

- Challenging the 'norm'
- Conversational intelligence that earns trust
- Establishing clear guidelines

R esults

- Focussing on collective results
- Establishing and maintaining momentum
- Relationships that drive outcomes and well-being

A ccountability

- Commitment from individuals, team/s and stakeholders
- Seeking and offering effective feedback
- Communicating with clarity, confidence and charisma

V ision

- Think it, act it, feel it
- The team that re-wires - inspires
- Looking good and feeling even better

E xtraordinaire

- Modelling best practise
- Being your best everyday
- Team legacy and beyond

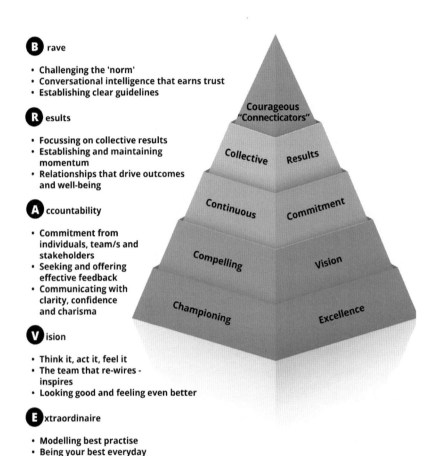

Courageous "Connecticators"

Collective   Results

Continuous   Commitment

Compelling   Vision

Championing   Excellence

Technology is constantly disrupting today's business models, and is often where teams can fly in the face of existing thinking.

I am working with lawyers who are digitalising their business so that their clients will have access to an online portal, where they can understand everything going on without having to speak to a lawyer. They are working toward property transactions completing in days, not months. They are being disruptive, putting the customer first, as they realised most people don't like talking to lawyers. The better the question, the better the answer. "Do they need to speak to us?" was the disruptive question, as traditionally, time is money for lawyers.

Get your team to brainstorm disruptive questions. Work on creating a safe, *one-team* environment (Sometimes clear guidelines are required on when and how), to support and encourage each other to challenge the norm and strive for success. A team of **courageous connecticators** will unleash together what's possible.

The ability to ask disruptive questions happens better and faster when leaders can create a team spirit of partnership, and focus on **collective results and championing excellence.**

These days, more than ever, a **challenging-the-norm** mindset helps to shape an extraordinary team.

In a fast-paced, changing world, today's norm is tomorrow's history.

When Lewis Hamilton clinched his fourth Formula 1 world championship for Mercedes, in 2017, he said, "I really want to say a big thank you to all the guys at Brixworth and Brackley. Guys, thank you for all your hard work."

The 1,500 people at Brixworth and Brackley were the 1,500 reasons why this team were champions. Together, they kept the ball up for years in a row: team members, who pushed everyone hard intellectually; drivers; people who worked their fingers to the bone, day in and day out, to create the tools and resources. They had the best driving pair in Formula One, and the best team of people behind them all the time.

They all pushed each other to new levels, always *challenging the norm*. When they thought they couldn't go any faster, they somehow found another tenth of a second. They wanted their team legacy to be part of history, so they each brought their best every day.

Collective results and championing excellence, drive (literally!) them all every day!

Big businesses that think boldly and act confidently will create opportunities for success.

What *norm* should your team challenge? Challenging them all is a good start but not always practical. What's most crucial?

Accountability is crucial to have **continuous commitment** from the team.

Having clear team guidelines, as to how you as a team will act, is a worthwhile investment of a team's time—even if it's a newly formed team.

The legacy of one of my client's teams, who are working on a huge people transformation project, is Awesome Programme – Fantastic Team. Before they had this, they were not connecting well, as they were newly formed and had been brought in after the programme had already hit some hurdles. They were defending their own territories and not focusing on collective results.

In one day, we did some powerful work on them, getting to know each other personally and professionally, which helped them *push past politeness quickly* (one of the day's objectives).

They had to agree to not let their egos slow them down, and to realise their opinion was not always right. Through facilitating a **circle of trust**, they understood their enormous breadth of skills, experience, strengths and weaknesses. They agreed best ways of working together to hit the ground running as a high performing team.

Every day, they promised to care, and to be connected, committed, and confident.

Importantly, they held each other accountable to consistently demonstrate their agreed promises.

Once at their best, they realised that they demonstrated continuous commitment and supportive challenge, and would listen, learn, and improve. After that day, they went on to embody their core values and ways of working to effectively communicate key results and activities to stakeholders, and the programme was a success.

Successful teams crucially have a **compelling vision**, one that excites everyone to go beyond potential into what's possible.

A great example of a leader's articulated vision was when President John F. Kennedy, in 1961, challenged Congress and the American nation to land a man on the moon by the end of the decade.

You may have heard the story of President Kennedy visiting NASA headquarters for the first time. He met the staff and asked them what they did. The janitor/caretaker replied, "I'm helping put a man on the moon!"

When everyone is thinking the vision, feeling the vision, and acting the vision, the vision happens. I believe that the team that rewires (behind their vision), truly inspires everyone around them. Remember, a vision must be 8 words or less!

The magic is when not just teams but companies instil this approach and stop working in silos.

Unfortunately, what I have often witnessed is that, the larger the company, the slower they have been in encouraging this to happen.

Teams end up working separately and extremely hard to strip cost from the business, instead of working together to serve their clients, make customers' experiences better, and generate more business.

So, as a leader, ask yourself, "Who is your team?" People who report to you are your team, project groups are teams, your peers in the business are your team, and department heads are a group team. Companies focusing on a one-business team approach, I believe will be more successful.

The world is moving at a faster pace than ever before. Our knowledge is doubling every 13 months! This is generally too fast for individuals to make much headway on their own. Leaders who do not prioritise building a high performing team will get left behind. Focusing on collective results together creates momentum, pace, and great synergy.

From the world of sport, we can learn a few lessons from Alex Ferguson's leadership at Manchester United, where he made it clear that no one was bigger than the team. The team had their greatest success under his leadership. He eagerly spotted talent and nurtured it from within. He turned exuberant players, such as 17-year-old Ronaldo, into team players. Part of Fergie's genius was to make everyone understand that glory and riches flow from being part of a winning team. He also believed in what was possible and, in his mind, focused on winning. He famously said, "I've never played for a draw in my life."

To remind you, when he became manager of Manchester United, in 1986, the tough reality was that the side had not won the football league for 26 years, and he was worried about the players' levels of fitness and alcohol consumption.

His approach was simple: Increase discipline, and see improved results.

He tackled problems head on and did not allow them to fester, which commanded loyalty as a true father figure.

Alex Ferguson stayed true to these values while continuously developing his style and systems. He excelled in managing multi-generational succession at his club. At the time, that style worked, but times have moved on. Fergie ended up mellowing, as the modern player seemed somewhat more fragile than when he started. It is teams, rather than just leaders, who now need to display these same characteristics.

To boost a team's self-belief, a leader with the WOW factor must learn to master the skills of:

- Finding and nurturing the greatness in others.
- Strengthening the capacity for human compassion and creativity in a stressful environment.
- Knowing when to empower and when to lead.
- Demonstrating amazing resilience.
- Staying *connecticated* with your team.
- Tackling poor performance quickly.

You can use your knowledge of people, including their DiSC profile, so you can help them be their best more consistently. Leading by example, at your best, really helps them with this, as does sharing your stories, your experiences, your learnings, and your mistakes - simply just being human.

Be really tuned in to what motivates them and what matters to them. Leaders who foster and build strong relationships, and understand what reinforces people, strengthen their ability by using positive reinforcement in a meaningful way. Show you care through nice gestures; maybe it's buying them their morning coffee or organising an event. We spend a lot of time at work, and most people work hard. Be human—ensure people have breaks and get fresh air. Maybe have team meetings outside. Non-tangible reinforcements are also vital to connecting: Interact with people, show interest, and take time to have a useful conversation or find out what they would like to get involved in. Make sure feedback is given regularly and in an appropriate manner. Depending on their style, D's like feedback straight away; I's love public praise; S's appreciate thanks and praise, particularly when they do something new/different; and C's prefer feedback to be given privately and with notice.

What can you and your team do to contribute to the bigger picture?

You must continually demonstrate **strong leadership**. In particular, take time out to communicate to stakeholders and all other business teams. When teams live their purpose together, they quickly create an environment for success.

Involve people, emphasise communication, and keep them in the loop. When teams step up and act as an example of accountability, they have a greater chance of getting support when there are obstacles.

In a team, be an **opportunity creator**; don't wait for things to happen—go and make them happen. There are opportunities for success—for you individually and for your teams—to do great things, to shine, and to stand out.

Your influence as a WOW leader is paramount to team success, business success, and your personal success. Your ability to connect and communicate with people, through clear compelling visions and strategies that everyone understands and believes in, will mean that people will want to work with you and for you. Your teams will be the ones people want to work in because they know that there is a spirit of partnership and unity; and it is going to be valued and reinforced, and there is a true climate of mutual trust.

Your Next Actions

What could you do to strengthen unity in the team?
How much do you do together that is not work related?
When did you last thank each team member individually and tell them what you appreciate about their contribution?
How could you make team meetings more exciting and productive? Could different team members lead them?
Whom could your team collaborate with across the business?
What successes/learnings could your team share with colleagues?
What team activity would be good? Ask your stakeholders about best tips for high performing teams.
Is your team on message? If not, Team Pulse is required!

Secret 3 - the second W in WO**W**

What's Most Crucial?
Being your best self is the most critical leadership quality you
can bring every day.

Chapter 9

Know Your Best

Best - adjective — (desirable type or quality) the highest standard or level that someone or something can reach.

"Real leadership is less about seeking applause and rewards, and more about doing the best work you've ever done, and having an impact you've never imagined."
– Robin Sharma

In today's world of constant information, many of us feel overwhelmed. Our clients in our coaching and training programmes struggle to switch off. They think too much. Their minds are full and rarely mindful. They are busy *being busy*, instead of busy being their best.

We need to train our brains to be our best.

As I listen to my clients, I hear clues as to how their brains work, from how they speak.

I pay particular attention to what comes after the words, *I think, I feel, I know.*

I will often ask them questions about what they feel, think, and know, and it's very powerful in helping them understand how to be their best self.

Often, when we feel overwhelmed, we overthink. When people are overemotional, they overfeel. Often, regretted decisions are made quickly, without time to think through the consequences, or without considering how you or others might feel.

If you feel that you or others are overemotional or overtired, try not to make a decision. Sleep on it, and decide the next day. Yes, it is possible, a lot of the time. Lead at your best.

As I introduced in Chapter 3, as a guideline, I believe that leaders with the WOW factor, at their best, act on 20 per cent what they think, 40 per cent what they feel, and 40 per cent what they know. It's what can be described as using your head, heart, and gut.

Scientifically, it's using your brain more harmoniously. It results in action and emotion, achieving purposeful objectives.

If I can borrow from the notions of Dan Siegel (clinical professor of psychiatry at the UCLA School of Medicine, and executive director of the Mindsight Institute), his work on brain integration derives from understanding that our brain has three different states of energy processes, which together create how the mind works.

State 1 is Rigidity. It only has one task, which is to stay *as is*.

Often, clients who display this state will say something like, "They are who they are, and they haven't done badly so far."

State 2 is Chaos. Clients often come in telling me about the multiple initiatives they are running, the challenges they are firefighting, their travel round the country or the world, and their lack of sleep or lack of time to do what they want. Their busyness often leads to a lack of clear communication to their teams, a lack of empathy or awareness of what is going on for team members or their boss, and very little effort in stakeholder relationships.

When we can lead ourselves, we are so much better equipped to lead others.

When our brains are more harmonious—Dan Siegel calls it *the river of integration*; I prefer to call it *the river of possibilities*—we can be our best.

Dan Siegel and his friend and colleague, David Rock, created *The Healthy Mind Platter*, seven daily essential mental activities to optimise brain matter and create wellbeing.

This creates *harmony* for our brain to function at its optimum, so we can be our best.

Focus Time: When we closely focus on tasks in a goal-oriented way, we take on challenges that make deep connections in the brain.

Play Time: When we allow ourselves to be spontaneous or creative, playfully enjoying novel experiences, we help make new connections in the brain.

Connecting Time: When we connect with other people, ideally in person, and when we take time to appreciate our connection to the natural world around us, we activate and reinforce the brain's relational circuitry.

Physical Time: When we move our bodies, aerobically if medically possible, we strengthen the brain in many ways.

Time In : When we quietly reflect internally, focusing on sensations, images, feelings and thoughts, we help to better integrate the brain.

Down Time: When we are non-focused, without any specific goal, and let our mind wander or simply relax, we help the brain recharge.

Sleep Time: When we give the brain the rest it needs, we consolidate learning, and recover from the experiences of the day.

In a society that is seeing an increase in burnout and mental health problems, never has it been so important to nourish our mental wellbeing each day.

We are all much better informed about what foods and food groups are good for us. It is equally important that we know what's good for our brain too, so that we can be our best.

When we understand how our brain works and how we can be at our best, then we can help others to do the same. It's the secret power in having the leadership WOW factor.

Understanding and *using* this knowledge really does help you to elevate your impact, influence, and career.

As a leader, you have followers—show the way; be the way.

Dan Siegel and David Rock's advice on optimising *The Healthy Mind Platter* is: *"We're not suggesting specific amounts of time for this recipe for a healthy mind, as each individual is different, and our needs change over time too. The point is to become aware of the full spectrum of essential mental activities, and as with essential nutrients, make sure that at least every day we are bringing the right ingredients into our mental diet, even if for just a bit of time. Just as you wouldn't eat only pizza every day for days on end, we shouldn't just live on focus time alone with little time for sleep. The key is balancing the day with each of these essential mental activities. Mental wellness is all about reinforcing our connections with others and the world around us; and it is also about strengthening the connections within the brain itself. When we vary the focus of attention with this spectrum of mental activities, we give the brain lots of opportunities to develop in different ways."*

One way to use the platter idea is to map out an average day and see what amounts of time you spend on each essential mental activity. Like a balanced diet, there are many combinations that can work well.

Work out what you need to balance to be your best. If you can work it out yourself, you'll be able to improve your relationships with your team, your colleagues, your family, and your friends.

Leadership can be lonely for many, and you need to discover what keeps you motivated, passionate, and in flow. Dan Siegel's guiding principles will get you into a place where you can consistently do that.

When have you been at your best? What were you doing? What was going on in your life at the time? How did it feel?

It is really important to notice and reflect on what triggers you to be at your best so you can try and recreate this more often. Of course, you cannot always be your best, but you can notice what gets you back there as quick as possible.

Maybe it's been when you are running regularly, or when you feel closer to loved ones, or are having regular sex. Perhaps it's connecting with nature or enjoying your favourite glass of wine.

Often, catching up with friends or reliving happy memories is good for us, as is planning new memories, such as booking a holiday, or reaching out to someone and letting them know you were thinking about them—you might make their day.

I am writing this chapter in my garden, enjoying the hottest day of the year so far.

I know I am at my best when I feel the sun on my skin. It totally lifts my mind, body, and soul. So do Fridays—I always say to myself, "Well done," on a Friday, no matter what's happened in the week. It's another week survived, and I've hopefully helped my clients, my kids and myself thrive!

For me, getting out in the sun as often as possible, and being free from distractions, is a must—both of which are difficult when living in the UK, being a single mother of three kids, and running a business.

A few years ago, I was keen to write a new course, create a new corporate brochure, and write an article (setting myself big challenges also keeps me at my best). I kept putting it all off—it was wintertime, and I was *busy*. I knew I wasn't being my best.

I decided to book three days in Lanzarote to help. Once booked, the pressure immediately eased.

When I got on the plane (and had my first drink in hand), my mind cleared, and I managed to design a new course outline on the flight going over.

After an afternoon in the sun, sipping a cocktail or two, my ideas for the brochure came together in a couple of hours.

The article still challenged me. Writing my thoughts always does!

It was my first article. I asked Niall, a family friend and journalist, for some tips before I left. He suggested that answering some questions on my topic might work.

I had kept looking at the questions and having brain freeze, so I switched off and went for a walk to explore the surroundings. Your subconscious works on what you need it to, without you thinking.

The next day, after a morning of sunbathing and swimming, I looked at the questions again and could answer them all. The answers formed the structure of my article.

I spend a lot of time helping my coaching clients create conditions for themselves to be at their best. Going on a spontaneous trip or being in the sun may not be what gets you at your best, or it may not be something that's possible for you to do, but like I mentioned, it's about working out what works for you.

One thing that is clear is that feeling stressed does not help.

Our 2 million-year-old brain has survival software. We're wired to look out for danger. This was very useful when we were likely to be hunted, and is, of course, still useful on occasions.

We unconsciously scan for safety, four times a second!

What's wrong is always available to us. What's right is different to this survival software. Decisions you make—and what I help my coaching clients do—can change your life and will free you. Make a real decision, not a preference or an "I'll try". If you just say this, you give yourself a way out, and your brain will try and keep you safe, and you'll suffer as a result. Make it a non-negotiable decision.

Being your best is about making great decisions in the *river of possibilities*, and acting on them.

Pippa, one of my clients, came into her first coaching session in quite a chaotic state. She'd been working extremely hard, putting in long hours, and had two young children. She felt her career was stagnant. By the time she got home most evenings, she was tired and would rush the children's bed times, so she could get to bed too.

One of the early decisions Pippa made was to spend more quality time with her kids, and that was her first *recalibration*. She felt much better after a week. She felt their love and they felt hers. This led to her listening more and having more honest conversations with colleagues and her team. We worked on how she allocated her time in the week and how she re-charged, and she managed a two-week secondment into another part of the business to broaden her experience and elevate her profile.

In her own words, "I plugged the holes in my boat, got the oars going in the right direction, and then managed to sail in the wind." She was sailing in the *river of possibilities*.

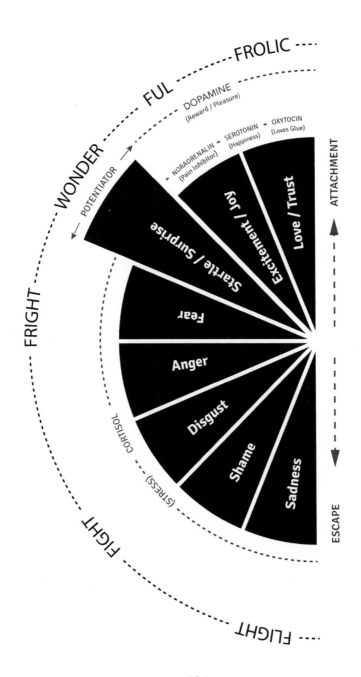

You need to startle/surprise your brain to take you from a place of stress.

The Be Brave diagram was something I co-developed with Catherine Doherty from Fields of Learning from some insights working with Professor Paul Brown, Professor of Organisational Neuroscience at Monarch Business School, Switzerland.

The diagram shows how the brain develops on demand in the *river of possibilities*, whereas stress shuts it down.

We have 8 basic emotions.

Fear, anger, disgust, sadness, and shame are the emotions in which the brain releases adrenaline, cortisol, and norepinephrine, the three major stress hormones, which together prompt a *fight or flight* response. When strong emotions such as these take over, our rational thinking shuts down.

Love/trust, excitement/joy, and startle/surprise are more positive emotions, with the startle/surprise element being a potentiator (to what's possible). In these emotion states, instead of your brain releasing cortisol—which is not conducive to you being your best—you will release hormones that make you feel happiness (serotonin), pleasure (dopamine), love (oxytocin), and even less pain (noradrenalin).

We need to think about spending more of our time in the positive emotional states, and less time in the ones that cause us stress. It can be a simple question that you ask someone or yourself, if they or you are stressed: "What's the one thing I can do right now to change my emotional state?"

Simply a change of scenery might work, whether it is going to get a coffee, going for a walk, making a phone call, taking a different route to or from work, or maybe going out for lunch with a colleague. Give pleasure to someone else by giving a hug, a kiss, chocolate, or flowers, or by having cakes for the team or telling them all to go home early. Do something different. Try something different, and find new ways of getting yourself to your best. Your brain then re-calibrates and gets comfortable with 'potentiating.'

Take some time off, even half a day. Meet or visit a friend/partner or family member for lunch. Pick up your kids from school and spend some quality, undistracted time listening to their day. Ask good, *connecticating* questions, not "'How was your day?" What is it you'd really like to know? I've had great conversations just by asking better questions: "What was your best bit today? What did you learn? Anything not so good today?"

Be curious. Reach out to someone you admire, or even to someone you don't get on with that well but whom it would be beneficial to befriend—perhaps a peer, or potential stepchild or in-law—and be the initiator of the start of a relationship.

Or be brave, and do something that scares you. I have even tried jumping out of a plane to test out this theory of our brain keeping us safe!

I love to learn from experts, and then I love to go a step further and challenge whether they are right. I was curious if I could keep myself calm enough to jump out of a plane—something that terrified me. I did some research (to appease the left-hand side of the brain) on which skydiving companies were best respected and seemed most professional. It may sound silly, but I explained to my brain that this was a multi-million-pound industry that also had vested interests in keeping me safe. The instructors were confident, clear, and well drilled in training us for our first jump. It took less than an hour, as it was a tandem jump— basically, if we did exactly what we were told we would be safe. I did manage to keep myself calm, and as we went to a height of **13,000 ft. (almost 2 miles)** over Suffolk, I still felt calm and positive. As my bottom edged precariously to the open door of the plane, and I leaned back very closely into my instructor's body, securely attached, I looked up to the sun and still felt relatively successful in keeping calm. I can definitely tell you that our brains are wired to keep us safe, because as we jumped (we fell at about 120 mph, descending to 5,000 feet in around 40 seconds), the reptilian (oldest) part of my brain was screaming: "What the hell are you doing? You just jumped out of a plane, and you are the single mother of three kids!"

However, seconds later, the parachute opened, and the quietness, the scenery, and the feeling of pure calm that took over was incredible. This was a startle/surprise in action.

After jumping out of the plane, and understanding how being brave is so good for you, I then bought my daughter, for her 16th birthday, and for my godchildren's 18th and 21st birthdays, a tandem jump. Their faces were a picture when they simultaneously opened their voucher. They were fearful and then nervously excited about doing it together.

As the plane disappeared into the clouds, and before I saw their parachutes appear, again I thought, "Oh, my goodness, I love these kids more than life itself; what have I done!"

It's hard to go past fear—but sailing in the river of possibilities lies in being brave.

They were ecstatic at their achievement. Three months later, I asked them if it had made any difference to their lives. Mikayla, my daughter, said yes, and that she felt like anything was possible. Jack, my godson, who was doing his Physics PhD, and also played Gaelic football, said he noticed that after the jump he felt much braver generally, and how he called for the ball a lot more. They were rewiring their brains themselves—like magic! It really boosted their confidence and go-getting attitudes, and they all now believe in what's possible. Mikayla decided on an internship in Germany, living on her own at 18, and is now living in Barcelona for a year.

It made me realise that the earlier anyone realises this, the better. You may find some team members less resistant to being brave, so maybe get them on board and contributing first in meetings when you are exploring what's possible.

I am also a great believer in it never being too late for anything. One of my favourite stories is about a 104-year-old man who decided to emigrate to NZ. The journalist asked him why he was doing it now, and he replied, "I don't want to regret it when I am 105." Anything really is possible.

In leadership, your resilience will often be tested.

The American businessman, Arnold Glasow, said, "One of the tests of leadership is the ability to recognise a problem before it becomes an emergency."

When we are no longer able to change a situation, we are challenged to change ourselves.

Again, when it's hard to be your best, remember the *river of possibilities*. Make a decision and take action.

My daughter started university last year, and I missed her dearly. She's my friend, my confidant, and my partner in crime.

My two teenage boys, at home, were really pushing the boundaries.

My ex-father-in-law, who the kids and I were close to, passed away suddenly at Christmas.

It was a tough, emotional time, and I knew I was not acting, thinking, or feeling like my best.

I had to get back to my best as quick as possible for all our sakes.

I knew I had to startle/surprise myself, so I decided to write this book, create our online WOW Your Presentations programme, and plan a round the world trip, combining holiday and business, for a global book launch.

I got the kids involved and excited, and our family energy changed.

We went from "I am sad" to "I feel sad"—a monumental shift.

"I am" are two of the most powerful words in the dictionary— what comes after them affects your mind and makes it more rigid. Saying to myself, "I am going to write this book," kept me believing it was possible.

It is easier to change your mental state when you tune into the feeling you are experiencing. It's okay for us to feel sad and to know why.

It was also okay for us to do things to make us feel happy. We gave ourselves permission to be more flexible, in the *river of possibilities*.

My sons also decided their goals. We planned a holiday, so we had something to look forward to. Charlie decided to aim for a try in every rugby game he played. Cameron took his first steps in his aspirations to become an Architect by securing some relevant work experience.

Take notice of what works to help you be your best, and what doesn't, and be courageous and try something new. Never give up on being your best. It's contagious to others—it works with your family, your team, and your colleagues.

As a leader, you must. Being your best will inspire others, and they will inspire you.

Being at your future best is sometimes about identifying gaps.

What are your gaps?

When people are promoted, they are least likely to think of their knowledge/skills gaps.

You should always be mindful of these, and showing ways you are trying to improve.

For example, if you are not digitally up to date, ask someone, who is, to mentor you, or even to reverse mentor you. If you are clear on why you need to learn (to improve my impact, to understand P&L accounts), what you want to get out of it (to be more confident presenting in larger forums, to confidently contribute in financial conversations), and how long you want it (for an hour/a day/once a month over a coffee), and you then tell someone that, they will usually say yes.

You can also ask an HR colleague for support in this area.

Sometimes being brave is about admitting what you don't know.

I asked Mark, a KPMG partner, what it meant to him to become a partner. He said it was like being part of a rugby team.

He had people (other partners) he could call when he wasn't sure.

Sometimes being brave is about asking for help. It's okay not to know.

Who do you know in your company, in your network or in your friendship group that may have been through similar challenges?

They may not have the answer you need, but something they say could spark an idea that helps you.

Could you get an informal focus group across the company to brainstorm an idea or challenge that you have thought of?

For some people, being their best is about commitment: committing to something, taking action toward it every day no matter what, and seeing it through to get the desired solution, or even bettering it.

For some people, being at their best is stopping and reflecting instead of charging ahead.

For some people, being brave is about identifying their gaps and not trying to cover up weaknesses. Leadership is about continually growing. If it's technical skills you lack, book yourself on a course, start reading about it, do some research, or reach out to experts for their knowledge.

Could you network more, even if it scares you? We are wired to connect as humans. It makes us feel good to talk to people, and you can use your Pulse if asked what you do!

Could you say yes next time you are asked to speak at something; or better still, could you offer?

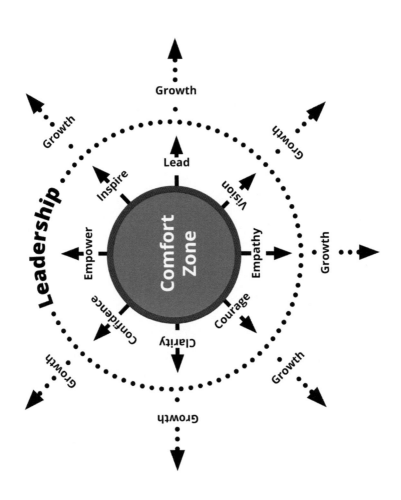

Who do you really need to listen to and then have an honest conversation with, to move a situation forward?

Perhaps you could benefit from having a mentor. I always ask my coachees whether they have a mentor, and rarely is the answer yes. Get support in choosing one if available. If there is no support, then go about getting one yourself. My steer would be to pick someone who is not similar to you.

They should be good at what you find challenging, and help you to stretch/grow out of your comfort zone. Think about how to approach them asking for their support.

Using the pulse questions for structuring your conversation should help.

What's the purpose of this mentoring? *Could you mentor me to be better at stakeholder relationships?*

How is this person uniquely placed to support you? *I admire your reputation and your relationships across the business.*

What's your vision for the mentoring? *I want to increase my influence and profile across the business.*

What's your suggested strategy? *Could we informally chat once a month for 6 months?*

What will the legacy be? *I'd like to be confident and comfortable with a wider variety of stakeholders.*

If you are very clear on why you need a mentor, why them, and for how long, nine times out of 10, they will say yes.

Reverse mentoring is also worth considering. To get digitally upskilled, perhaps you could buy lunch for someone in your IT department for a couple of months, and they could share with you the latest technology, app, or trend.

Being aware of your best, your gaps, your stretch, and your development points, and doing something about it, is much admired in your leadership journey. You will grow and be in a much stronger position to help and inspire others.

You then have a new best to build on.

Getting regular feedback during your career, ideally from a wide range of stakeholders, is really useful to get some perspective on your leadership and development.

I would recommend asking a red, an amber, and a green stakeholder.

Red is someone who knows you a little.

Amber is someone who perhaps you have worked with before or more recently on a project.

Green is someone who champions you.

What is it that you want feedback on? Be specific with what you ask them—in person, by phone, or by email. Give them a heads-up so they have time to reflect. It could be general feedback; for example, "What do I do well? What could I do more of? What should I stop doing? Or more specific, "What do you think is holding me back? How would you describe my leadership style? What's the one thing I need to work on to improve my personal brand?"

Or ask your team, "What's the one thing that I could do more of to help you?"

Feedback feeds growth and helps you be your best.

Do this, and repeat it throughout your career to have the leadership WOW factor.

Be passionately committed to what is possible. Be courageous. Be your best.

Next Actions

When have you been at your best? Maybe get some feedback by asking a mixed variety of current colleagues (and boss) and past colleagues (and bosses), and perhaps selected family and friends.

What were you doing? What was going on in your life at the time?

Could you recreate this or something similar?

Whom could you get feedback from? What do you want the feedback on?

Whom could you reach out to, in your support network, with a current challenge?

What are your development areas?

Who could mentor you?

What do you need to do more of to be your best?

What distracts you from being your best? How are you going to prevent this?

What one thing can you make non-negotiable to keep you at your best?

What can you do/say to get yourself back on track when you have a wobble?

Chapter 10

Know Your Priorities

*"The key is not to prioritise what's on your schedule,
but to schedule your priorities."*
– Stephen Covey

As I said at the beginning of this book, what has got you to this level is not usually what helps you excel, and can also hinder progression to the next level, especially at the top of the corporate ladder.

In my time with clients, we work out what they should keep doing, and more importantly, what they should stop doing, what they should do more of, and how to discover new skills to help navigate the ladder gap, such as adapting behaviour, improving personal impact, and increasing influence.

Hopefully, from earlier chapters, you can begin to understand what difference that can make.

If you have been following your next actions, you will already be feeling and seeing the difference.

The definition of *crucial,* which I like, is: "Decisive or critical, especially in the success, failure, or existence of something."

This resonates because how you decide the importance of your career determines the success, failure, or existence of it.

Many talented people work really hard at their jobs, but not many work hard at all at their careers! So, decide how crucially important your career is. You spend enough hours involved in it.

You've read this far into the book. I now wish I could time travel with you, a year or two into the future, and grab some of the confidence and WOW factor you will have, bring it back, and give it to you to use now. I have seen, time and time again, how leaders are unleashed when they decide to focus on their career and not their job. It benefits them professionally, personally, and emotionally—they really do have the WOW factor.

When I'm working with my coaching clients, we work each month on the last element of the WOW factor:

What's most crucial? What are YOUR priorities? It's vital that you ask yourself those two questions.

Your head is potentially sabotaging your progress if you stay too busy being task related, or more likely, managing, not leading.

Do you need to pay attention to your partner/kids/alcohol intake/exercise regime/wellbeing/connection with friends?

Do you need to be spending more time with your direct reports in the next few months so you can develop them, so you delegate more to them in three months?

Do you need to be collaborating better with another part of the business?

Do you need to spend time on relationships?

Do you need to broaden your perspective?

Could you be seconded to another part of the business?

Do you need a coach/a mentor/upskilling/technical training to address a development area?

Could you collaborate with another company to offer something game changing to the market?

Do you need to develop your pipeline?

Do you need to spend more time with your clients/customers?

Do you need to adapt your style more often?

Do you need to get your reds to ambers, and ambers to greens, on your stakeholder orbit spreadsheet?

Do you need to work smarter, not harder?

Is there a better question you need to ask yourself than the ones above?

Working on your priorities will move you forward.

Success and happiness come from moving forward.

Care jointly about your career and your job, moving forward together.

Keep a sharp focus on the bigger picture—YOUR VISION—and prioritise tasks that move toward it.

Act on those tasks, delegate, have the needed and difficult conversations, get support, and overcome those obstacles.

Move forward, every day, toward your vision as a leader and your life vision.

Move forward with your learnings. If things go wrong, learn from them. Share those learning experiences—it's where you instil vulnerability and trust.

Move forward with your relationships. Connecticate with people and build trusted relationships.

Move forward with your development. What are your gaps? What are you going to do about it?

Move forward even when it's scary. As Richard Branson says, "If someone offers you an amazing opportunity, and you are not sure if you can do it, say yes—then work out how to do it later." Be brave!

Move forward with your team, and create a team spirit of partnership.

Move them all forward with their development. Make sure you have developed your #2 so that when your next opportunity or promotion is available, there's no reason for them to say no.

Ownership—remember, it's Y.O.U.R. career—own it!

Your Impact, **O**rbit Effect, **U**rgent Career Priorities, **R**epeat! This is not something you decide to spend a few days or months on. It's something you continue to work on. If you are, by any chance, reading this slightly sceptically, that's the C-style coming out in you! Don't worry; as I say to my clients, "You can't not know all this now!" So, even if you disagree with something—perhaps because it's not relevant now—it might be one day. It will already be in your subconscious, and you may not remember you read it in this book, but you will know what you need to do. Or come back every few months to this book and rate yourself out of ten on each of the chapters and work on what you need to do next to get yourself closer to a ten. You should never reach it though – there's always something you can do even better!

Own your career. Be the driver of your career, not in a pressured way—just check in by getting on all your balconies and observing where you are. Then just ask yourself, "What's most crucial?"

Own your reputation. Honour your word when you say you'll do something, and get it done well and as quickly as you can. Successful leaders keep their word and their promises. Ensure people know you mean it when you say it; this way, people will trust you, trust what you say, and be more likely to work with you and for you, and champion you.

Own the wellbeing of your body and mind. Regardless of how busy you are, always take time to do what you love doing. Some of my clients realise they have not done what they love for a long time. Like I said in Chapter seven, do what keeps you at your best; it's a priority. Maybe it's getting weekly date nights back in your life, or making the effort to meet up with some good friends. Have your favourite meal with a favourite bottle of wine. Get involved with your kid's football team, dance, sing, pick up that guitar, take up your favourite sport, spend one-on-one time with someone important, book an event, take a country walk, and have a pub lunch.

What do you love doing? What brings you joy? It is critical that you find this time.

This is what your memories are made of. Taking time out clears your head of its challenges, and the solutions will come to you. It turns off your thinking and allows your experiences and knowledge to recalibrate, to know and feel the right way forward. It helps you feel alive, relaxes you, and makes you more resilient.

I know you may already know this, but do you do it enough? The people that don't, or put it off, week after week, get stressed, sick, and burnt out. Just carrying on is not sustainable, and you'll be a nightmare to live with, work with and be with.

When you are feeling and being alive, and not being a robot, it vitalises the people around you.

Be both responsible and accountable for your quest and its outcome. Be kind to yourself.

Trust that if you do this, everything will work itself out in the right way, at the right time (even though it may not feel like it).

What do you need to make non-negotiable?

Own your focus. Wake up every day or decide the night before, what's most important to get done today, and do it! You will achieve more and be happier.

Sound judgement is a key strength; trust yourself more.

Intuition and reason come first (heart and gut) over facts and experience (get away from your head controlling you).

You have the courage and ability to make decisions free of prejudice, egos, or emotions.

Trust yourself more, and others will trust you.

Choose what is right for YOUR organisation; have the mindset of a business owner.

Show courage and drive to lead.

Nathan was leading a £50 million two-year digital transformation for his company. One year in, they realised it was much more complicated than they thought, and they needed a lot more collaboration throughout the business than they had planned.

He requested that an emergency board meeting should be called.

He presented and said that they should invest in some expert advice, and that the whole programme should be reset. He thought he may get sacked, as that would put the programme over budget. However, he was determined to do what was right for the business, and was thinking like a business owner. The board, though initially shocked at his suggestion, soon realised it was the right decision long-term, and got advisers in to help reset the programme. Nathan was asked to stay on to lead the programme, which was a success and projected £150 million savings over three years.

He was clearly motivated by doing the right thing for the long-term sustainability of the firm, and displayed integrity at all times. Nathan became COO of the company, 18 months later.

What's most crucial for you now? You tell me. Your gut and heart already know. Don't overthink it.

Remember, humans at their best should be 40 per cent knowing, 40 per cent feeling, and 20 per cent thinking.

It's generally when you do your best work. We can all get over emotional, overthink, or act on our instincts without thinking it through or how it will affect others.

Many of the people I coach generally have been overthinking and not trusting themselves enough.

The leadership WOW factor is bringing together the principles of: know your message and be your message; know your impact; know your stakeholders; know your style; know your influence; know your team; know your best and know your priorities.

These are summarised into the three secrets that you should reflect on:

- **W**hat's your impact/message?
- **O**rbit effect
- **W**hat's most critical?

This approach is not difficult, but it does take effort. The effort pays off; where focus goes, energy flows! It literally is like career magic dust—all sorts of things begin to happen to join your future career dots. You being at your best consistently really does unleash the leader within.

Your PULSE as a leader, and/or in your current role, will be your compass to get you there.

You need to decide what ACTIONS you will take, and you will need to be a bit braver and try things outside your comfort zone. As I mentioned in Chapter nine, your brain is wired to keep you safe, and it has kept you safe to get you to this point. But it will also keep you there. To get to the next stage of your career, you need to decide: what action, decisions, and bravery will you take? Or will you continue to do what you have done that keeps you safe and comfortable every day?

Remember that the other side of being brave is love, fun, excitement, and trust.

Trust yourself because, **when you trust yourself, others trust you too.**

History is full of leaders with extremely different leadership styles: a quiet and simple Ghandi; a soft-spoken peanut farmer named Jimmy Carter, who became President of the United States and won a Nobel Peace Prize; a loud and flamboyant Churchill or *The Iron Lady*, Margaret Thatcher.

There may be a few leaders you admire whose behaviours you may use as reference points, but never copy or imitate them.

Generally, in large corporates at a senior level, often just below the top jobs, people slightly lose their uniqueness and understanding of why they were taken on in this role. Don't try to fit in—it keeps you stuck. You are born to stand out! Yes, you!!! Be yourself.

We all have different leadership styles, and the key is to *Be Your Best Self*, and move forward.

You only have one reputation, and combined with great relationships and great results, success will naturally follow.

As Winston Churchill said, *"A pessimist sees difficulty in every opportunity. An optimist sees the opportunity in every difficulty."*

Be Brave. Be Great. Be You.

I wish you the very best of luck in your career and would love to hear how you get on.

Feel free to drop me a line anytime to tara@leadershipwow factor.com.

If you want any additional on-line support, you can also message me at the same address.

Next Actions

What are your priorities?
What do you need to move forward?
What areas need your attention?
What most needs your focus?
Where do you need to be brave?
What's most critical, right now, today? Tomorrow? This week? Next week? This month? Next month? This quarter? Next quarter?
Reflect on your achievements regularly, and keep track of them going forward.

Next Action Notes

Next Action Notes

Next Action Notes

Next Action Notes

Next Action Notes

Next Action Notes

Next Action Notes

Next Action Notes

Next Action Notes

Next Action Notes

Next Action Notes

Next Action Notes